WHAT MANAGERS
SHOULD KNOW
ABOUT AUTOMATION

What Managers
Should Know
About Automation

Charles E. Silberman

AND THE EDITORS OF *Fortune*

HARPER & ROW, PUBLISHERS

New York, Evanston, and London

Contents

Illustrations

Preface

"The great enemy of truth," the late President Kennedy suggested in his 1962 commencement address at Yale University, "is very often not the lie—deliberate, contrived, and dishonest—but the myth—persistent, persuasive, and unrealistic." Few myths have been more persistent, persuasive, and unrealistic than those concerning automation and technological change. This book attempts to separate the facts of automation from the myths.

To do this is no easy matter. Man's relation to his technology —to the tools and concepts through which he extends his capabilities—has always been a fertile subject for myth-making. The machine in general and the computer in particular seem to touch some raw nerve, some irrational and deep-rooted fear—a fear reflected in the universal popularity of the Frankenstein and Golem legends of man-made robots who turn on their creator. (The late Norbert Wiener drew on the legend of the Golem to explain his own fear of the computer, to whose development he contributed so much.) In the ancient myths, man generally remained master of his own fate, though at the price of the loss of innocence. In the contemporary myths, man becomes the servant of his own instruments; his *hubris* in trying to build to the sky leads to loss of livelihood or, worse yet, loss of freedom and autonomy.

These grim myths of automation gained strength in the early 1960s because the spread of the computer happened to coincide with an extended period of unemployment; 5 to 6 percent of the labor force was out of work—a socially intolerable figure. It was tempting, and superficially plausible, to point the finger of guilt at automation. Those who, in another of President Kennedy's memorable phrases, like to "enjoy the comfort of opinion without the discomfort of thought" were quick to do so. As a result, more and more people were misled into believing that the United States had entered a new and frightening era in which automation was robbing human beings of the means of earning their daily bread, thereby condemning vast numbers, particularly the unskilled and poorly educated, to idleness and uselessness.

This book grew out of my concern about unemployment and my puzzlement over its apparent intractability; I felt that the extent of joblessness was socially and morally unacceptable, but I was unconvinced that automation was the villain. Hence I requested and received from the editors of *Fortune* a broad charter to study how automation and new technologies were affecting the labor market and, through it, American society and culture. I have long felt that journalism and scholarship, far from being antagonists, require each other—that indeed one cannot deal satisfactorily with the larger and more insistent problems of the present except through some merger of the two disciplines. Thus the research, which got under way in the spring of 1964 and continued through the spring of 1966, combined economic and statistical analysis with journalistic probing—interviews with businessmen, trade unionists, workers, and scholars; visits to factories and offices, employment services, and schools; and unending debate with my colleagues and myself.

The result was a series of seven articles, reprinted here substantially as they appeared in *Fortune* over a span of seventeen months, from January 1965 to May 1966. (I was responsible for six of the articles; my colleague, Edmund K. Faltermayer, wrote the seventh, included in this volume as Chapter 4.) I have rewritten the text only where necessary to update the statistics and to eliminate repetition or topical references that may have lost their point. The substance is unchanged; the events of the past eighteen months have only served to vindicate arguments which, at the time I advanced them, were attacked as outrageously wrong or complacent, or both.

Those arguments may be summarized fairly briefly.

1. *Automation is not a significant cause of unemployment, in large part because there isn't much automation.* The amount of automation already in place, and the rate at which it is likely to grow, have been wildly and irresponsibly exaggerated by social commentators and critics who confuse what may be with what is. These myth-makers fail to distinguish between what is scientifically possible and what is economically feasible. The fact is that scientists and engineers can perform almost any task demanded of them; but they can perform comparatively few at a price the civilian economy can afford.

This is not to deny that technology is changing; clearly it is. Nor is it to deny that such change displaces substantial numbers of workers; clearly, it does, and, equally clearly, the displacement is often painful. But the fundamental question raised by the new myth-makers of automation is not whether technology is changing, nor whether such change causes hardship, nor even whether that hardship should be alleviated. The question, rather, is whether technological displacement is occurring at a rate so fast as to erect a technological barrier to full employment. The answer—now clearly confirmed by the sharp drop in unemployment in late 1965 and the growing concern about a "labor shortage" in early 1966—is that it is not. The rate of technological change has accelerated in the postwar period, but the acceleration is well in line with the long-term trend. (See Chapters 1 and 7.) In any case, what is crucial is not the absolute rate of innovation or of labor displacement but the relation between that rate and the rate of economic growth.

2. *New technology is exerting far less impact than had been assumed on the kinds of work men do and the amount of education and skill they need to do it.* Far from going out of style, for example, blue-collar work has enjoyed a strong and impressive comeback in the last several years. (See Chapter 2.) The long-run trend, of course, is away from the work of the hands and toward the work of the mind, but the movement is slow and gradual. Unskilled and semiskilled jobs, particularly of the manual labor variety, are frequently a lot harder to automate or even to mechanize than professional or technical jobs. And in the short run, the rate of economic growth determines the industrial and occupational distribution of the jobs that are available as well as

their total number. For the same reason, the much-worried-about crisis of teenage unemployment never materialized; employers have a marvelous capacity to adjust their requirements to the supply of labor that happens to be available. (See Chapters 3 and 7.)

3. *Man is not losing control of his instruments; technology is not taking over, nor is it effacing human will.* (See Chapter 6.) This is not to say that technology is neutral; it is not. Technology directly affects the choices open to the individual and to society in a variety of ways, most importantly, perhaps, by affecting our concepts of the good, the true, the beautiful. Modern technology, moreover, puts the problem of choice in a different context by removing many of the traditional constraints of time and place. The result is to enlarge, not to restrict, the sphere of human action and choice.

One of the choices can, and indeed, must be to alleviate poverty in the United States. The question is how. The American poor are not "immune to progress," to use Michael Harrington's phrase. Between 1959 and 1965, using the Social Security Administration's new definitions of poverty (about $3,100 a year for an urban family of four), the number of people living in poverty declined by about 6.5 million; the proportion of the population living in poverty dropped from 22 percent to 17 percent. In short, rapid economic growth does reduce the number of poor. But not rapidly enough—hence the wide agreement that the government should be waging war on poverty. There is some real question, however (see Chapter 5) as to whether the war can be won in the way it is now being fought.

My debts are many and great. The greatest is to Judith Wheeler of the *Fortune* research staff. Her relentless curiosity, her sensitive eye for the small detail that reveals the large idea, and her concern for the meaning as well as the formal accuracy of words and concepts, facts, and figures made her a collaborator rather than a research assistant. This book is hers as well as mine.

I am profoundly indebted, also, to Daniel Seligman, Assistant Managing Editor of *Fortune,* who edited the articles with great wisdom, sensitivity, and humor. The book owes much to his uncanny ability to detect what I was trying to say—and to help me say it with far greater clarity and grace than I could muster on my own. My debt is large, too, to Duncan Norton-Taylor, formerly Managing Editor of *Fortune* and now a fellow-member of its Board of Editors, who gave me the freedom and resources to spend six months following my journalistic and scholarly instincts before committing a single word to paper; and to Louis Banks, his successor as Managing Editor, who encouraged me to broaden the scope of the series still more. I am deeply indebted as well to my colleague, Edmund K. Faltermayer, the author of Chapter 4, who carried out the difficult task of working within another writer's framework with characteristic professional skill and aplomb. I am grateful, too, to Evelyn Benjamin of the *Fortune* research staff for her assistance on Chapter 4; to Brooke Alexander, Assistant to the Publisher of *Fortune,* who arranged for publication of the series in book form and who handled all the tedious details connected with publication with unending patience and good humor; and to Mrs. Barbara White, my secretary, who managed to keep some semblance of order in the compost heap that is my office.

In the course of researching and writing this book, I picked the brains of more people than I can possibly thank here. I am particularly indebted, however, to Alan Greenspan, president of Townsend-Greenspan & Co., consulting economists, for his insights into managerial economics as well as his statistical help; he developed the measures of productivity used in Chapters 1, 2, and 7 and of the changes in teenage occupations used in Chapter 3, and he acted as economic and statistical consultant throughout. I owe a large debt as well to Dr. Joseph S. Zeisel, Deputy Assistant Director for Research of the Office of Manpower Policy, Evaluation, and Research, U.S. Department of Labor, who gave unstintingly of his knowledge and expertise on a host of matters, large and small; to John Bregger of the Department of Labor, who provided vast amounts of published and unpublished BLS statistics, to Dr. Thomas M. Stout, formerly of Bunker-Ramo, now president of Profimatics Inc., and to Walter Doyle of Texaco, who helped separate the facts from the myths about the uses of computers in industrial processes; to Professor Peter F. Drucker of New York University, Professor Herbert A. Simon of Carnegie Tech, and

John Bailer of The Miehle Co. for their insights into the economics of automation; to Drs. Joseph N. Froomkin and A. J. Jaffe of Columbia University's Bureau of Applied Social Research for giving *Fortune* access to their unpublished analyses of occupational changes in the United States during the 1950s; and to Dr. Arthur M. Ross, Commissioner of Labor Statistics, for giving us access to a number of unpublished BLS and Labor Department memoranda and worksheets.

I should like to express my thanks, also, to a number of other people who gave generously of their time and knowledge: Jack Alterman, Herbert Bienstock, Richard W. Boone, Edgar S. Cahn, Warren Haggstrom, Stanley Lebergott, Sar Levitan, Lawrence A. Mayer, Marshall McLuhan, S. M. Miller, Daniel P. Moynihan, Charles Nowacek, Martin Rein, Murray Wernick, Albert Wohlstetter, Seymour Wolfbein.

My debts to my wife, Arlene Silberman, are larger and more profound than I can possibly express. Without her, nothing is possible; with her, everything is possible.

Charles E. Silberman

Mount Vernon, N.Y.
June 1966

1

The Real News About Automation

ONE OF THE MOST SENSATIONAL PIECES of news about the performance of the United States economy in this era of radical change and dire prediction is contained in a statistic that has been ignored by all but a handful of Labor Department economists. The statistic is this: Employment of manufacturing production workers increased by one million in the three and a half years from the first quarter of 1961 to the third quarter of 1964 and by another 700,000 by the fourth quarter of 1965. This increase dramatically reversed the trend of the preceding five years, when 1,700,000 production-worker jobs were eliminated and "the work of the hands" appeared to be going out of style. Such work is very much in style now.

This turnaround in blue-collar employment raises fundamental questions about the speed with which machines are replacing men. It was the large decline in blue-collar employment in manufacturing during the late 1950s and early 1960s, more than the persistence of high over-all unemployment rates, that persuaded so many people that automation was rapidly taking hold, condemning the unskilled and the poorly educated to a vast human slag heap. "The moment of truth on automation is coming—a lot sooner than most people realize," the Research Institute of America warned its businessmen-subscribers in December 1963. "Cybernation," said the sociologist-physicist Donald N. Michael, who coined the term (to refer to the marriage of computers with automatic machinery), "means an end to full employment." The Ad Hoc Committee on the Triple Revolution, a diverse but influential group of private citizens, went even further: in its view "cybernation" means an end to *all* employment, or almost all. Unless "radically new strategies" are employed, the committee warned President Johnson in March 1964, "the nation will be thrown into unprecedented economic and social disorder." It argued that "cybernation" makes a mockery of any attempt to provide jobs for either white or Negro workers. Technological change—the most crucial of the three revolutions the committee is concerned about (the other two are in civil rights and military weapons)—is creating an economy in which "potentially unlimited output can be achieved by systems of machines" requiring "little cooperation from human beings."

Nothing of the sort is happening. Two years of field research and economic and statistical analysis by *Fortune* make it clear that automation has made substantially less headway in the United States economy than the literature on the subject suggests. Fifteen years after the concepts of "feedback" and "closed-loop control" became widespread, and ten years after computers started coming into common use, *no fully automated process exists for any major product in any industry in the United States.* Nor is any in prospect in the immediate future. Furthermore, the extent and growth of several partially automated processes have been wildly exaggerated by most students of the economy. There is, in fact, no technological barrier to full employment.

This is not to deny that technology is changing; clearly it is. Nor is it to deny that such change displaces substantial numbers of workers. Technological innovation is always doing that, and it is always painful to the individuals directly affected—the blacksmiths, harness makers, and coachmen whose jobs were destroyed by the automobile, and the insurance-company clerks now being displaced by computers. But the question raised by Michael, the Research Institute, and the self-appointed Committee on the Triple Revolution is not whether innovation causes displacement of labor. It is, rather, whether technological displacement is occurring at a substantially faster rate than in the past—at a rate so fast, in fact, as to threaten a crisis of mass unemployment similar to that of the 1930s.

The view from Brooklyn

The answer is no. Automation, in any meaningful sense of the term, is only a minor cause of unemployment. The auto workers in South Bend who lost their jobs when Studebaker shut down, the packinghouse workers thrown out of work in Chicago and Kansas City when the meatpackers decentralized their slaughtering operations, the coal miners in Appalachia made idle by the loss of coal's biggest markets, the shipyard workers whose jobs ended when the Navy closed its yard in Brooklyn—all are in trouble and many are in need of help. But they are no more the victims of automation than were the New England textile workers of the 1920s, made idle when the cotton mills first started moving south, or the southern cotton pickers of the 1930s and 1940s, thrown on relief when the mechanical cotton picker came into use.

To the men in question, of course, this fine distinction may seem brutal and irrelevant: what matters to them is not the particular reason they are idle but the poverty—of the spirit even more than of the body—that idleness causes. But to those concerned with relieving and preventing unemployment, the causes *must* be central. There can be no greater disservice to the unemployed—indeed, no greater act of contempt—than to substitute easy slogans for ruthless honesty in analyzing the causes of their joblessness, and thus to fail to ease their plight.

There are two kinds of pitfalls in trying to understand an age like ours. One is to take comfort in some such platitude as "the more it changes, the more it stays the same," thereby underestimating or ignoring altogether what might be termed "the cosmic changes" going on. The other is to become so enamored of the cosmic—to focus so completely on all the possibilities of contemporary science and technology—that one loses sight of the realities of the present. Too many of the people writing about automation and "cybernation" have fallen into the latter trap: they have grossly exaggerated the economic impact of automation. At the same time, curiously enough, some of them may have underestimated or simply ignored its psychological and cultural impact. For technology—*any* technology—has a logic of its own that affects people more or less independently of the purpose for which

4 THE REAL NEWS ABOUT AUTOMATION

the technology may be used. The assembly line, for example, dictates a particular organization of work and a particular set of relations among workers, and between workers and managers, whether the line is turning out automobiles, breakfast cereals, or insurance-company records (see Chapter 6).

The importance of imitation

A good deal of the confusion over what's happening stems from a failure to distinguish between what is scientifically possible and what is economically feasible. For technological change is *not* purely a matter of invention, of scientific or technical capability— a fact most defense contractors have had to learn the hard way. On the contrary, as mathematical logician Albert Wohlstetter of the University of Chicago puts it, technological change "has to do with such grubby matters as costs, and uses, and competing purposes: in short, with politics, sociology, economics, and military strategy." Indeed, the great economist Joseph Schumpeter used to argue that invention per se played a relatively minor role in technological change. What was crucial, he insisted, was "innovation"—the process of finding economic applications for the inventions—and "imitation," his term for the process by which innovation is diffused throughout the economy. The time lag between these three steps may have been truncated by the growth of industrial research and development and by the growing recognition that knowledge is the most important form of capital. But a time lag does remain, and it can be substantial, as the disappointingly small civilian fallout from military and space research and development activities attests.

We have misunderstood what is happening, moreover, because discussions of the future of science and technology have turned into "a competition in ominousness," as Wohlstetter describes it. In their eagerness to demonstrate that the apocalypse is at hand, the new technocratic Jeremiahs seem to feel that any example will do; they show a remarkable lack of interest in getting the details straight and so have constructed elaborate theories on surprisingly shaky foundations.

To explain how automation is revolutionizing the structure of production and of employment, for example, Professor Charles C.

Killingsworth of Michigan State University told Senator Joseph S. Clark's Employment and Manpower Subcommittee about Texaco's computerized petroleum refining unit in Port Arthur, Texas, which, Killingsworth said, processes "several million gallons of raw material daily." He picked a poor example; the installation actually demonstrates how small the bite of automation is, and how large and numerous are the obstacles to its rapid spread. The unit in question produces about 80,000 gallons a day, 0.6 percent of the refinery's total throughput. The computer installation has been successful, to be sure. But the payoff has not come in reduced employment—the number of workers remained at three per shift for the first two years, at which time productivity gains unrelated to the computer enabled Texaco to cut the number to 2.5 men per shift, a net loss of two men. (Killingsworth told the Clark committee that it was his "guess" that the computer had "replaced a half dozen men in the control room.") The payoff has come, rather, in the greater efficiency with which the unit converts gases into polymers. More to the point, this particular process was picked for computerization because it was "relatively simple when compared with other refinery processes" and because it was one of the few processes for which good historical data (essential if control is to be shifted from people to computers) was available.

Since the first installation Texaco has put a second computer in control of some of the operations in a large catalytic cracker; the number of workers on this process has remained unchanged.

Killingsworth's mistakes about the capacity of the original computerized refinery unit and his exaggeration of its significance typify most of the literature on automation. Donald Michael's influential essay, "Cybernation: The Silent Conquest," published in 1962 by the Fund for the Republic, contains several other such exaggerations. One of them, having to do with the TransfeRobot manufactured by U.S. Industries, is discussed on pages 23–25. Michael's other examples also tend to dissolve under close scrutiny. Two examples:

Michael goes to some lengths to show how "cybernation permits much greater rationalization of managerial activities," e.g., "The computers can produce information about what is happening now . . . built-in feedback monitors the developing situation and deals with routine changes, errors, and needs with little or no intervention by human beings. This frees management for attention to more basic duties." Michael instances "an automatic lathe . . . which gauges each part as it is produced and automatically resets the cutting tools to compensate for tool wear." The lathe "can be operated for 5 to 8 hours without attention, except for an occasional check to make sure that parts are being delivered to the loading mechanism." This description of the lathe came from 1955 testimony before a congressional committee by Walter Reuther, who in turn was quoting from *American Machinist* magazine. Michael's reference to the lathe is almost a complete non sequitur. For one thing, whatever its impact on the machinists in the shop, it did not affect managerial activities at all. For another, no computer was involved. The machine was simply an improved version of a standard automatic lathe that machine-tool manufacturers had been making for several decades.

To show how cybernation permits rationalization of management—in this instance by "combining built-in feedback with a display capability"—Michael also cites the Grayson-Robinson apparel chain's use of a computer to handle "the complete merchandise and inventory-control function." Actually, the chain had neither "feedback" nor "display capability." It did use a computer to give management a weekly report of sales and inventory, but Grayson-Robinson merchandise men did all the buying and reordering. Perhaps the chain would have been better off if the computer *had* handled "the complete merchandise function," for it started a bankruptcy proceeding in August 1962 and was declared bankrupt in November 1964.

The anonymous ghosts

Not to be outdone by Michael's invention of the word "cybernation," the consultant, Alice Mary Hilton, president and founder of something called the Institute for Cybercultural Research, has coined the term "cyberculture" to describe the new "age of abundance and leisure" that computer-run factories will soon be forcing everyone to enjoy. Writing about the "cybercultural revolu-

tion" in the fall 1964 issue of the *Michigan Quarterly Review,*
Miss Hilton offered a few original examples of her own:

"In Texas and New Jersey, in the oil refineries—the silent,
lifeless ghost towns of this century—crude oil is processed into
different grades of gasoline and various byproducts—the propor-
tions determined automatically and flexibly as consumers' demands vary. Crude oil is piped in—gasoline and byproducts
emerge, hour after hour, day after day, without pause for sleep or
rest or play, without coffee breaks or vacations, sick leaves or
strikes. *There are no workers, no supervisors, no executives; just a
few highly trained engineers standing by in the central control
room,* watching their brainchild fend for itself." (Emphasis
added.) Unfortunately, Miss Hilton is closely guarding the identity
of these refinery "ghost towns." In Port Arthur, Texas, however,
the Texaco refinery alone employs 5,000 people, the Gulf refinery
4,000.

Computers are producing fuel for human consumption as well
as for machines, according to Miss Hilton. "In a Chicago suburb,
in a bakery as large as a football field," she wrote, "bread and rolls
and cakes and cookies are produced for millions of households
throughout the country by a team of machines, called a system
. . . *All the blue-collar and white-collar workers—of all levels—
have been replaced by a silent machine system that labors twenty-
four hours every day* . . . The bakery runs itself; the system even
maintains itself," her awe-struck report continued. *"The few
human beings still inside the 'black box' are only nursing the infant
cybernation to maturity."* (Emphasis added.) Miss Hilton presumably was describing the Chicago bakery of Sara Lee, a subsidi-
ary of Consolidated Foods. An elaborate computer system does
indeed control the blending of the ingredients and part of the
baking process to ensure uniformity of product, but people are still
required to perform a wide range of activities—e.g., braiding
Danish pastry dough and spreading chocolate icing. And, "the
few human beings still inside the 'black box' " come to about 450
per shift—300 of them in direct labor.

Walter Reuther, from whom Michael took his example of the

automatic lathe, has provided other instances of the devastating impact of automation. Appearing before Senator Clark's sub-committee in May 1963, Reuther compared the production methods used when he went to work for Ford in 1927 with those now in use. Once it took three weeks to machine the engine block for a Model T; in Ford's "automated" engine plant in Cleveland, which Reuther had visited after its opening in the early 1950s, the machin-ing took only 14.6 minutes, because "the technology in that plant is built around computers." He added, "The thing we need to understand in order to grasp this revolutionary impact of such technology is that this automated engine line . . . is already ob-solete."

Indeed it is. The engine line Reuther described was taken out three years before he gave his testimony—but not, as he suggested, because the computers it was "built around" had already become obsolete. On the contrary, the factory had no computers at all. The engine line was taken out because it was just too inflexible; when Ford redesigned its engines in 1959–60 it had to rebuild almost the entire Cleveland factory.

Caught on the horn of prophecy

The view that computers are causing mass unemployment has gained currency largely because of a historical coincidence: the computer happened to come into widespread use in a period of sluggish economic growth and high unemployment. Thus it was natural that some who were not looking too closely at the evidence would attribute the unemployment to computers and automation and would assume that a lot more automation must mean a lot more unemployment.

One of the first to push the panic button was W. H. Ferry, vice president of the Fund for the Republic. In a widely publicized essay entitled "Caught on the Horn of Plenty," published in January 1962 and still being distributed, Ferry stated flatly that "The United States is advancing rapidly into a national economy in which there will not be enough jobs of the conventional kind to go around." He then proposed a test: "The next three years ought to suffice to determine whether a liberated margin [his term for the 'technologically displaced'] is in fact in the making. If by 1964 the unemployment rate is close to 10 percent, despite the use of all conventional medications, we may be ready to agree that once again, as in the Thirties, the nation is in a radical dilemma, a dilemma of abundance."

The three years have passed. The unemployment rate did not rise to 10 percent, as Ferry believed it would; instead it declined from its high of 7.1 percent in May 1961 to 4.9 percent in November 1964 and then it proceeded to drop still more—to 3.7 percent in the spring of 1966. In part, of course, the decline in unemployment in 1965 and 1966 was a side effect of the rise in defense spending associated with the war in Vietnam, and unemployment could rise again if defense spending were cut. But to compare our situation with that of the 1930s, when 13 million people—25 percent of the labor force—were unemployed, is to indulge in reckless distortion. The persistence of high over-all unemployment and the changes in the occupational structure of the labor force during the 1950s and early 1960s were due less to automation or technological changes than to a combination of quite different (and in some instances, quite temporary and reversible) economic forces. These are analyzed in detail in Chapter 2. The remainder of this chapter will examine what in fact *is* happening to productivity and consider why automation has proceeded so much more slowly and has had so much less impact on employment than so many had expected.

The sources of productivity growth

If technology were in fact threatening mass unemployment, the threat should be reflected in an acceleration of the rate at which productivity—i.e., output per man-hour—is increasing. What *has* been happening to productivity? Do the statistics of output per man-hour show any evidence of revolutionary changes in the structure of production? In general, the rate of productivity increase tends to accelerate over time, for productivity feeds upon itself. For the last 115 years, however—about as long a period as we can measure—the acceleration has been gradual, averaging about 0.2 percent per decade. Gross private (nongovernmental)

Chart 1. Long-Term Productivity Growth in the Private Economy

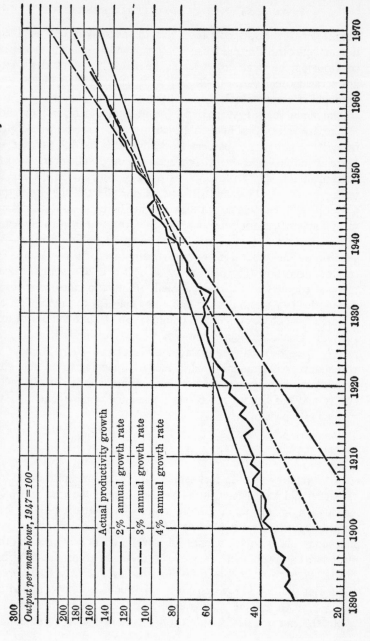

Output per man-hour, 1947=100

Actual productivity growth
2% annual growth rate
3% annual growth rate
4% annual growth rate

output per man-hour grew at an average rate of only 1.3 percent a year between 1850 and 1889.* The average jumped to 2 percent during the next thirty years (1889 to 1919), and then to 2.5 percent between the two world wars. Between 1947 and 1960 productivity gains averaged 3.3 percent a year; since 1960 the annual increase has averaged 3.6 percent.

The productivity gains these last five years, it should be pointed out, are running ahead of *Fortune's* 1959 forecast of a 3.4 percent average annual increase for the 1960s as a whole—a forecast that most academic and business students of productivity dismissed at

* Gross *private* output (rather than gross national product) per man-hour is used because it is impossible to provide a meaningful figure for productivity of government employees.

An acceleration in the growth rate of productivity is no new phenomenon, as so many enthusiasts of automation seem to think. On the contrary, the rate has been accelerating for a hundred years or more. (See Chart 1.) Between 1850 and 1889 (not shown), gross private (i.e., nongovernmental) output per man-hour grew at an average of 1.3 percent a year. The rate jumped to an average of 2 percent a year between 1889 and 1919 (thick line), and then again to 2.5 percent between the two world wars. Since 1947 productivity gains have averaged 3.4 percent a year, and just since 1960 3.6 percent a year. The straight lines' show what the productivity index would have been had the rate averaged 2, 3, or 4 percent a year.

The chart also helps to place the recent spurt in productivity in historical perspective. It has always grown irregularly, with many spurts and lags. The spurts, of course, are concentrated in years of sharply rising output; the secular gains are more apt to reflect changes in technology, industrial organization, and education. Thus, increases of the sort realized during the first half of the Sixties have been experienced before and have usually been followed by periods of productivity lag. Between 1920 and 1924, for example, output per man-hour shot up by 4 percent a year as the assembly-line and other mass-production techniques gained wide acceptance. In the next five years, however, the rate dropped by more than half. Later, in the six years following World War II, productivity advanced by 3.7 percent a year, but then slowed to an average of only 2.5 percent in the following seven years. Obviously, it is too soon to conclude that the recent 3.6 percent a year rate of productivity growth will last.

the time as extravagantly optimistic. But note several things about these large productivity gains: Even larger gains have been registered over comparable or longer periods a number of times in the past—for example, from 1920 to 1924 and 1947 to 1953. More important, such figures reflect a lot more than technological change. Firms increase productivity, for example, by making their employees or their machines work harder; by hiring employees with more education or training, or by giving employees on-the-job training; by changing the way in which work is organized (e.g., using a typing pool instead of individual secretaries); or by changing the product "mix" (making more high-priced products).

It is inherent in the way productivity is measured, moreover, that above-average gains are recorded during periods of rising output and below-average gains during periods of stable or falling output. Productivity had been held down from 1955 to 1960, partly because output itself had been very sluggish, partly because the huge capital expenditures of 1955–57 and the enormous buildup in R. and D. activities had both, so to speak, diverted manpower from current to future production. When the boom finally got under way in 1961, therefore, business had a reservoir of new products and new production processes to draw upon. More important, almost every industry had some excess capacity, which meant that until mid-1964 or thereabouts, firms could fill incoming orders using only their newest and most efficient facilities. They could also concentrate their capital expenditures on equipment designed to increase the efficiency of existing facilities rather than spending to increase capacity. In addition, high unemployment rates made it possible for employers to be very choosy about whom they hired. Taking everything together, there are good reasons for viewing the productivity gains of the past few years as not entirely sustainable for the rest of the decade. In fact, the productivity rise did slow down in 1965 to 2.8 percent, from 3.6 percent the year before (see Chapter 7).

If the Triple Revolutionists were right—if we were in fact developing "a system of almost unlimited productive capacity"—it would follow that business firms could realize substantial increases in production without having to spend very much on new plants and equipment. But the current business expansion has triggered

Chart 2. Postwar Productivity Growth by Industry

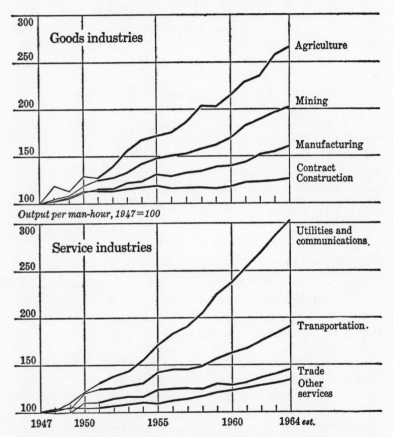

Talk of the over-all rates often tends to blur the widely divergent trends from one industry to another. For all the talk about automation, output per man-hour has increased more slowly in manufacturing than in the economy as a whole since 1947—i.e., by 2.9 percent a year vs. 3.4 percent for the economy. These recent gains in manufacturing are barely half as large as those realized during the 1920s, when a real revolution in manufacturing technology was taking place.

the greatest capital-goods boom in history—considerably more than twice the size and duration of the capital-goods boom of the mid-Fifties.

Moreover, if a "new era of production" had really begun, it would have to show up in manufacturing, the most critical sector of the economy. Yet productivity has been growing a bit more *slowly* in manufacturing than in the economy as a whole. In the entire postwar period, manufacturing productivity has increased by 2.9 percent a year, vs. 3.4 percent for the private economy. There was an acceleration in the 1960–65 period, to be sure. But these recent gains in manufacturing were smaller than the gains realized in the decade following World War I, when technology was being revolutionized by the assembly line and the endless-chain drive. Between 1919 and 1929, output per man-hour in manufacturing increased by 5.6 percent a year. The acceleration in *over-all* productivity growth since the 1920s has come about because mechanization and rationalization have been applied elsewhere in the economy—e.g., in finance, insurance, retail and wholesale trade.

The brewmaster's nose

If there is not now any "cybernetic revolution" in manufacturing, perhaps there will be one soon. How likely is any such event? The answer seems to be—not very. Consider some obstacles that have been encountered in trying to automate continuous-process industries like oil refining, chemicals, and paper.

These industries looked like sitting ducks to manufacturers and designers of computer systems. They are characterized by enormous capital investment in processes in which relatively small increases in efficiency can yield large improvements in profit. By the mid-1950s they had actually gone pretty far toward automation. All that had to be done to achieve complete automation—or so it seemed at the time—was to substitute computers for the human beings monitoring the instruments and controlling the variables of the production process.

The next step was never taken; there are now about 400 process-control computers in use in the United States, but the essential control of the production process remains in human hands, and minds. Refineries and chemical plants, with their miles of pipes and tubes, and paper mills, with their gigantic machines dwarfing the handful of attendants, may *look* as though they are controlled by machines, but they're not. What is literally meant by "automation" or "cybernation," i.e., a process in which a computer or some other machine controls all aspects of the process from injection of the raw material to the emergence of the final product, determining the proper mix and flow of materials, sensing deviations from the desired operating conditions and correcting these deviations as they occur, or before they occur—we are a long way from all this. In the electric-power industry, for example, which has more than a third of all installations, computers are used mostly as data loggers, recording what happens in the process for the engineers to analyze and study. So far no more than a half dozen or so plants are using computers to control the elaborate sequence of events involved in starting and shutting down a generating station, and only a few plants are using computers to determine the optimum distribution of power throughout the system. In pulp and paper mills, computers serve primarily as data loggers.

Most of these industries have realized large gains in productivity in recent years. But the gains have come less from computers than from better material handling and from installation of larger and more efficient machinery of the conventional sort: for example, bigger electrical turbines and generators, bigger cat crackers in oil refineries, larger-diameter oil and gas pipelines, bigger and faster paper machines. The computers themselves have displaced very few people, if any at all, partly because computers are being used to perform functions that had not existed before; partly because the number of employees involved in controlling the process had already been reduced to the bare minimum needed to take care of emergencies. Computer manufacturers today try to justify their systems by pointing, not to savings in manpower, but to reduction in raw-material costs and increased efficiency in operation.

Full automation is far in the future because, as Peter F. Drucker has observed, "There's no substitute for the brewmaster's nose." The productivity of a paper mill, for example, hinges in large part on such things as a machine operator's ability to establish the proper "freeness," and this he does by watching the water "go along the wire." (The operator watches a mixture of water and fiber going past him; if he feels that the water is traveling too far before draining out, or not far enough, basic operating adjustments have to be made.) There is no *scientific* reason why such operations cannot be automated; in principle, the brewmaster's nose can be too, and in time it probably will be. But the costs of doing so are inordinately large, and the time inordinately long: no industry understands its production process well enough to automate without huge investments of time and capital.

Consider, for example, the basic oxygen process for making steel. The system designers discovered very rapidly that they didn't have data precise enough to enable them to set up a mathematical model describing what actually goes on in an oxygen converter— the first step in designing a computer-controlled system. The data were too crude because the instruments being used were too crude. And the instruments were crude because steelmen didn't know what quantitative information they needed—not because they were uninterested, but because before computers came along they had no use for more refined data. Hence the computer manufacturer must study the process long enough to determine what information is needed, then find instruments sensitive enough to yield that information in quantitative form, then hook up these instruments to a computer to monitor the process long enough to determine what happens and to identify the critical variables. Only then can it try to develop a mathematical model of what goes on in the process.

And setting up the model can be the most intractable job of all. It turns out, for example, that the mathematics of controlling an oxygen furnace, an oil refinery, or a paper mill are in some ways more complicated than the mathematics of controlling a missile or a satellite. The only mathematical technique now available for handling as many variables as are found in most industrial processes is "linear programing." Unfortunately, as Dr. Thomas M. Stout, a process-control engineer and consultant, says, "practically no relationships in nature are linear." Thus, designers of computer process-control systems have had to develop their own mathematical techniques as they went along.

Each new computer installation, of course, makes the next one easier; in time, computers will be able to control more and more production variables. The point is that the change will be gradual and that it will not lead to peopleless plants. The most fully automated refineries, paper mills, and generating stations now imaginable will still require a work force something like the present one. Even if computers could handle all the operating variables in a paper mill, for example, the number of operators probably would not be reduced below the present seven per machine. As one production man explains it, "at least fourteen hands are needed immediately to re-thread the paper when it breaks"—and the paper breaks an average of twice a day.

The elephants and the mahouts

The obstacles are multiplied several times over when firms try to automate the production of more complicated products that have to be assembled from a large number of parts. Automation, like mechanization in general, proceeds in two ways—either by taking over functions that men perform, e.g., substituting the automobile or the plane for man's feet, substituting the lever, the wheelbarrow, or the power-driven machine for man's arm and shoulder muscles; or by eliminating some of the functions that have to be performed, e.g., eliminating the setting of type through the use of punched tape, eliminating the thousands of operations that are needed to assemble an electronic circuit through the use of printed circuits. Changes that involve the elimination of functions may have great impact when they come—but they come very infrequently.

Most technological change, therefore, involves the mechanization of existing functions—what the brilliant Canadian student of technology, Marshall McLuhan, calls "extensions of man." Three broad kinds of function can be distinguished: muscle power or sheer physical strength; sensory-manipulative operations such as picking things up and moving them elsewhere or guiding a shovel to the right spot with the right amount of force (as distinguished from the exertion of that force); and problem solving, using the brain to analyze a problem, select and process the necessary information, and reach a solution. What distinguishes the computer from most previous technological innovations—what makes it so awesome—is that it can tackle the second and third of these functions, not just the first. This enormous potential of the computer is the kernel of truth—a very large kernel—that the Triple Revolutionists have got hold of, and that gives their arguments so much surface plausibility.

But when we try to apply this newest extension of man to the process of physical production, we start running into difficulty. Many kinds of gross physical activity have already been mechanized out of existence, or soon will be, by simple and relatively inexpensive means, such as conveyer belts, lift trucks, and overhead cranes. The odor of perspiration has largely disappeared from the factory and the construction site. Most of the people left in the production process are involved in sensory-manipulative operations like assembling automobiles or directing a steam shovel. And these tasks—relatively unskilled and uncomplicated as they may appear—are the hardest operations of all to automate.

In addressing a meeting some years ago on the theme "The Corporation: Will It Be Managed by Machines?" Professor Herbert Simon of Carnegie Institute of Technology, one of those working on the furthest frontiers of computer utilization, reflected on a tableau that had been enacted outside his office window the week before, when the foundations for a new building were laid. "After some preliminary skirmishing by men equipped with surveying instruments and sledges for driving pegs," Professor Simon observed, "most of the work [was] done by various species of mechanical elephant and their mahouts. Two kinds of elephants dug out the earth (one with its forelegs, the other with its trunk) and loaded it in trucks (pack elephants, I suppose). Then, after an interlude during which another group of men carefully fitted some boards into place as forms, a new kind of elephant appeared, its belly full of concrete, which it disgorged back into the forms. It was assisted by two men with wheelbarrows—plain old-fashioned man-handled wheelbarrows—and two or three other men who fussily tamped the poured concrete with metal rods. Twice during this whole period a shovel appeared—on one occasion it was used by a man to remove dirt that had been dropped on a sidewalk; on another occasion it was used to clean a trough down which the concrete slid." Simon concluded, "Here, before me, was a sample of automated, or semi-automated, production."

What the sample suggested was that automation is not, and cannot be, a system of machines operating without men; it can be only a symbiosis of the two. The construction site demonstrated another important fact: we may be further from displacing the eyes, hands, and legs than we are from displacing the brain. The theoretical physicist, the physician, the corporate vice president, the accountant, and the clerk, Simon suggests, may be replaced before the steam-shovel operator or the man on the assembly line.

Our versatile children

The reasons are partly technical, partly economic. The technical have to do with man's present superiority over machines in dealing with what Simon calls "rough terrain"—the uneven ground of a construction site, the variations in materials assembled in manufacturing, or the irregularities in the shape of letters, the sound of words, and the syntax of sentences. Man's versatility in handling rough terrain was never really appreciated until engineers and scientists tried to teach computers to read handwriting, recognize colors, translate foreign languages, or respond to vocal commands. The human brain turns out to be, as Herbert Simon puts it, a remarkably "flexible general-purpose problem-solving device." An adult can recognize over a million variations of the color blue. The merest child can recognize an "e" in upper or lower case, in italics or upright, in boldface or regular, in print or handwriting, in manuscript or cursive, and so on almost ad infinitum—and all of these in an almost infinite range of sizes, colors, thicknesses of line, etc. And he can catch the meaning of words spoken by a voice that is masculine or feminine, high-pitched or low, loud or soft, pronounced with an enormous variety of regional and foreign accents. In short, the central nervous system is an incredibly versatile machine.

Its versatility is equally great—perhaps greater—in dealing with activities involving the coordination of eyes, ears, hands, and feet. "Manipulation is a much more complex activity than it appears to be," Ralph S. Mosher of General Electric wrote in the October 1964 *Scientific American*—even the seemingly simple operation of opening a door. "One grasps the doorknob and swings the door in an arc of a circle with the hinge axis at its center," Mosher explained. "The hand pulling the door must follow an arc lying in a plane at the level of the knob parallel to the plane of the floor, and it must conform to the circumference of the circle defined by the distance from the knob to the hinge axis. In doing this the hand, assisted by the human nervous system, is guided by the door's resistance to being pulled along any other path. In other words, the human motor system responds to a feedback of forces that must be interpreted. A strong robot, lacking any means of such interpretation and free to pull in any direction, might easily pull the door off its hinges instead of swinging it open."

The complexity of the economic considerations that determine what to automate, and when, is shown in International Harvester's construction-equipment factory outside Chicago. One of the plant's three engine-block lines is "automated"—i.e., it employs numerically controlled machine tools to machine engine blocks for enormous earth-moving machines, which are produced in relatively small volume. (For any product produced in quantity, conventional machine tools are cheaper.) But the blocks are moved from one automatic machine station to the next by men, using a simple overhead crane. Right next to this automated line is a conventional machine-tool line turning out vast numbers of engine blocks for tractors and trucks. On this conventional line, first installed in the late Thirties, the engine blocks are moved from station to station by conveyers and other transfer devices. The reason is simple: the volume handled on the "automated" line doesn't justify the cost of installing and operating transfer machinery for a conveyer belt; it's cheaper to move the blocks by hand.

New jobs, old skills

Because it may actually be easier to mechanize or automate clerical, managerial, and professional work than the kinds of blue-collar work that still remain, current discussions of the labor market may be exaggerating the future demand for professional and technical workers and underestimating the future demand for blue-collar workers, a question examined in greater detail in Chapter 2. The discussions almost certainly overestimate the tendency for automation to upgrade the skill requirements of the labor force. "It is not true," Professor James R. Bright of Harvard Business School, perhaps the most careful academic student of automation in the United States, has written, "that automaticity— automation, advanced mechanization, or whatever we call it— *inevitably* means lack of opportunity for the unskilled worker and/or tremendous retraining problems." In some instances skills are up-graded; in some they are reduced.

Over-all, however, what evidence is available (and there's painfully little) suggests that automation does not radically alter the existing distribution of skills. *Jobs* change, all right, but not the level of skill, particularly as firms gain more experience with automatic equipment. When business computers first came into use, for example, it was generally assumed that computer programers needed at least a college degree. Today most computer users find a high school education adequate, and even this can occasionally be dispensed with. There is an enormous amount of repetitive work, moreover, under automation. The work may involve a different kind of rote, but it is still rote; it's hard to imagine a much more monotonous job than that of key-punch operator.

The crucial point is that we don't have enough experience with automation to make any firm generalizations about how technology will change the structure of occupations. On the one hand, automation may tend to *increase* the proportion of the population working as mahouts and wheelbarrow pushers in Herbert Simon's metaphor and to decrease the proportion working as scientists, engineers, technicians, and managers, because it may prove easier to displace people at these latter jobs than at the former. On the other hand, rising incomes will tend to increase the demand for services, in which jobs typically involve ill-structured problems and "rough terrain"; the demand for teachers, psychiatrists, journalists, and government officials, for example, is likely to expand faster than the demand for ditchdiggers or light-bulb changers. (The large increase in employment of clerical and professional and technical workers that has already occurred has been less the result of technological change per se than of the fact that industries employing relatively large numbers of such workers, e.g., insurance, education, medical care, have increased their output much more rapidly than industries employing relatively few. There has been relatively little change in the proportion of professional and clerical workers *within* individual industries. See Chapter 2.)

A question of costs

Sooner or later, of course, we shall have the technical capability to substitute machines for men in most of the functions men now perform. But the decision to automate would still be an investment decision—not a scientific decision. At any one point in time, businessmen may choose between a wide variety of combinations of capital and labor. Their choice is affected very strongly by the relative costs of capital and labor—illustrated quite clearly, for example, in the fact that International Harvester finds it cheaper to use men than conveyers to move the engine blocks from station to station on that "automated" engine-block line.

In the last analysis, men will not be replaced by machines because widespread substitution of machines for men would tend to reduce the price of the latter and increase the price of the former, thereby creating a new optimum combination of the two. At any given moment business firms will use capital, i.e., machinery, instead of labor in those operations where machinery's advantage over labor is the greatest, and they will continue to use men in operations where the machine's advantage is the least. For the last 150 years of constant technological change, with only rare exceptions, such as in the 1930s, capital and labor have managed to combine in the United States so as to keep 95 percent or more of the labor force employed. This has been a remarkable record, one that has made the United States economy the envy of the world. It would be premature to conclude that this record cannot continue indefinitely.

Meanwhile, if one focuses on a single industry, or a single plant, or a single process within a plant, of course, he can *always* find rather frightening evidence of technological unemployment. Consider this description of technological change in the steel industry, written by an English journalist after touring an up-to-date mill in the United States. "The thing that struck me first was how few men there were about," he reported. "To watch the way in which ingots were gripped from the furnaces, laid on rollers, carried on to be pressed, rolled out with steel fingers automatically putting them into position, you would have thought the machines were human." Even more impressive, the Englishman found, was the process for manufacturing steel rails: "From the moment the ore is pitched into the furnace until the rail [is] finished, everything is done by machinery, and *no man has a direct hand in the work.*" (Emphasis added.) The plant was the old Carnegie works at Homestead, Pennsylvania; the time of the visit was 1902.

U.S. Industries' marvelous mythmaking machine*

"To tell the truth about automation is not an easy task. Too many people are willing to accept too many myths," the late John I Snyder, Jr., president and chairman of U.S. Industries and a self-styled "pioneer" in the design and production of automation equipment, complained.

Indeed they are—and one reason is that Snyder himself, through his testimony before congressional committees, his frequent press releases, and his generous assistance to anyone interested in automation, contributed substantially to the cultivation of these myths. One contribution has been that darling of the science fiction writers, the robot —specifically, U.S. Industries' TransfeRobot, an inexpensive ($2,500) automaton capable of replacing people on almost any assembly-line task.

Or so a number of enthusiastic or frightened writers have reported. A close look at both the reports and the record helps explain why "the truth about automation" is so hard to determine.

In 1959 the New York *Times* reported the development of the TransfeRobot 200—"a new concept in automatic machinery designed to eliminate the dull, repetitive tasks of employees in small as well as large plants."

In 1960, Snyder told the congressional Joint Economic Committee that "we stand on the threshold of a new era in automation. As the earlier phase was dominated by the introduction of giant automated industrial complexes, such as refineries or engine plants," he amplified,

* This case study of one widely publicized piece of "automation equipment" provides a clear insight into the way in which at least some of the myths of automation are generated.

"the era which we are now entering will have as its distinguishing factor the introduction of small automation units into existing factories. In the past the industrial producer has had to go to automation. In the era we are entering automation will come to the producer." This new era, Snyder modestly explained, was made possible by U.S. Industries' development of the TransfeRobot.

In June 1961, the New York *Times* reported that U.S. Industries had developed "the first general-purpose automation machine available to manufacturers as standard 'off-the-shelf' hardware"; the report quoted Edwin F. Shelley, then a U.S.I. vice president, to the effect that previous automation devices had been for special purposes or custom-made. "The new machine, called a TransfeRobot," the *Times* continued—apparently forgetting that it had announced the development of the TransfeRobot in 1959—"has been in use some time under test conditions. Now it will be marketed for sale or rent."

In October 1961, the *Times* once again introduced its readers to the TransfeRobot. The occasion this time was the dedication of U.S. Industries' Silver Spring, Maryland, "Automation Center." "The star of the show," the *Times* reported, "was a self-perpetuating device, said to be the first of its kind in industry, called TransfeRobot 200, a registered trademark. It contains its own electronic guiding device and is said to be the first low-price, flexible, automation machine to be produced in quantity for use on any production line." At the ceremonies Shelley announced that "more than fifty TransfeRobot 200's have already been purchased by major companies for use on their assembly lines." This favorable response, he added, "indicates to us that within five years the probable annual market for such devices will total some $100 million."

In January 1962, Donald N. Michael published his widely publicized "Cybernation: The Silent Conquest," described by the *Times* as "a gloomy report of an automated world, in which people will be consigned to the junk heap." As evidence of the versatility of automatic machinery, Michael pointed, among other things, to the TransfeRobot 200, quoting that June 1961 *Times* article. Michael's quotation of the *Times* article was then reproduced in *Computers and Automation* magazine, and a reproduction of *that* reproduction turned up a few months later in a U.S. Industries promotional booklet. The U.S.I. press release that seems to have inspired that 1961 *Times* article had—to use a term that recurs in discussions of the miracles of automation—"closed the loop."

In a July 1963 article entitled "Automation: Its Impact Suddenly Shakes Up the Whole U.S.," *Life* reported that "almost anything that hands born of woman can do" the TransfeRobot "can do better, faster, more cheaply." "So far," Snyder was quoted as saying, "we have not been able to find any material or any shape or any size it can't handle."

The other thing Snyder was unable to find for the TransfeRobot was a real market. "I think you're on the wrong track," James H. Cassell, Jr., then U.S.I. public-relations vice president, finally told a *Fortune* researcher in September 1964 after she had tried for months to find out how many TransfeRobots had been sold. "You're pursuing something obsolete." The TransfeRobot, he admitted, had not been a good piece of equipment. Pressed again for sales figures, he guessed they had come to "twenty-four or twenty-five robots"—less than half the number claimed in 1961. Asked which corporations had bought the robots, Cassell said he would have to check and call back. An assistant made the call, explaining that the TransfeRobot 200 had been "marketed"— i.e., lent to potential customers on a trial basis—but that none had actually been sold in the sense in which that term is usually used.

Further digging by *Fortune*, however, turned up six customers that had bought a total of eleven TransfeRobot 200's. But none of the five firms willing to talk to *Fortune* have been able to use the TransfeRobot 200's successfully. One company never used the robot at all; in trial runs, the machine broke down almost daily. Another firm retired the TransfeRobot after six months, and a third is still tinkering with its robots in an effort to get them to perform up to specifications. *Fortune* did find a satisfied customer for the TransfeRobot 210, a later model. This robot, custom designed at a cost of about $10,000, displaced one man.

In any case, U.S. Industries, as still another of its public-relations spokesmen explained, is no longer "pushing the individual Transfe-Robot." ("If someone asked for one," he added hopefully, "we would sell it to him.") "The TransfeRobot as such is not functional," Cassell elaborated, "but what we learned from it is being used in our automation systems."

Sales figures on the "automation systems" also proved elusive. "We're concentrating 100 percent in the candy industry," Cassell explained in December 1964. As nearly as *Fortune* was able to determine, two or three such systems were on order, and one was actually in full operation—in the Smiles 'n Chuckles candy factory in Kitchener, Ontario. The $250,000 system handles about 30 percent of the factory's packaging. All told, Smiles 'n Chuckles employs, on the average, 385 people in the Kitchener plant, 85 of them still in packaging; U.S. Industries' system displaced 12 people.

2

The Comeback of
the Blue-Collar Worker

"THE GREATEST EVIL of unemployment," the late Lord Beveridge once wrote, "is not the loss of additional material wealth which we might have with full employment"; it is the fact that "unemployment makes men seem useless, not wanted, without a country." Unemployment, Beveridge went on to emphasize, should not be confused with poverty: "Idleness is a positive separate evil from which men do not escape by having an income." Hence no amount of unemployment insurance or relief can possibly offset the social destructiveness that long-term or chronic unemployment produces.

For all the prosperity of the past several years—and in retrospect it is clear that the Sixties have soared as advertised—the United States was not able to avoid the "evil of idleness" until very recently. To be sure, the situation has been improving, not deteriorating, much popular discussion of unemployment to the contrary. Between the time the current boom got under way in the first quarter of 1961 and the fourth quarter of 1964 nearly four million jobs were added, and the number of unemployed declined by one million. The unemployment rate dropped from the first-quarter 1961 average of 6.8 percent of the labor force, seasonally adjusted, to 5.0 percent in the final quarter of 1964. At this rate, 3,700,000 people were without any jobs; another two million were working part time because they could not find full-time jobs, and perhaps a half million more—some of them older men, some of them housewives, some of them youngsters in or out of school— would have liked to work but were discouraged from even looking for a job.* As might be expected, unemployment was not spread evenly throughout our society. The unemployment rate among Negroes was more than twice that among whites; the rate among blue-collar workers was more than double the white-collar rate. And teenagers had the highest rate of all: proportionately, three times as many teenagers as adults were out of work.

Some unemployment is inevitable, of course, in a free and dynamic economy. A certain number of people will be out of work so long as employers retain their freedom to fire and employees their freedom to quit or to turn down unsatisfactory offers while looking for a job, and others will be unemployed because of physical disability, mental illness or retardation, or plain laziness. The Bureau of Labor Statistics has estimated this unavoidable "frictional unemployment" to be about 3 percent of the labor force; that, at least, was the average for 1953, the last year during which economists generally agree that there was full employment. However, not everyone agrees that we should aim for a 3 percent rate (see Chapter 7).

On any standard, however, unemployment exceeded the acceptable minimum from the mid-1950s, when the rate hovered around 4 percent, until the winter of 1965–66, when it returned to that level. Unemployment rose to 7.5 percent during the 1957–58 recession and in the ensuing recovery got down only to 4.9 percent. Of the other major industrial nations, only Canada had more unemployment; in Great Britain, France, West Germany, Italy, Sweden, and Japan the rate had been running two-fifths to four-fifths lower than in the United States. (Despite a widespread view to the contrary, differences in the way unemployment is measured have very little to do with the bad showing of the United States. Had other countries followed the BLS definitions in 1962,

* These "invisible unemployed" may be offset in some small measure by those among the 3,700,000 who were not seriously interested in finding work and listed themselves as unemployed only to collect insurance; but BLS studies indicate their number is negligible.

for example, when the United States unemployment rate averaged 5.6 percent of the labor force, the rate would have been 1.8 percent in France, 2.8 percent in Great Britain, and 1.5 percent in Sweden.)

Why did it take the United States so long to achieve full employment? More important, what did this difficulty portend? What changes may be needed to keep us at full employment? The first chapter argued that whatever the causes of unemployment might be, automation was not one of them—that automation has made substantially less headway in the United States, and has had far less impact on employment, than the alarmist literature on the subject suggests.

The house of structuralism

But one need not be an alarmist to regard the duration of high unemployment, and in particular its concentration among the relatively uneducated and unskilled, with some foreboding. A growing number of people, in fact, have come to regard the apparent intractability of unemployment as evidence of some far-reaching changes in the structure of the economy and its technology. "Unemployment," says Senator Joseph S. Clark, chairman of the Senate Subcommittee on Employment and Manpower, "is a symptom of a broader and more fundamental challenge; it is part of a manpower revolution. We are moving from a blue-collar to a white-collar economy, one which offers fewer and fewer opportunities for the unskilled and the uneducated." In one variant or another, this "structuralist" view is shared by a remarkably diverse assortment of economists, businessmen, and government officials of both parties and all shades of political opinion. They view unemployment as the result of a growing disjuncture between the demand for labor and its supply. Some of them are oppressed by the automation specter, but all are concerned about technological change in general, including changes in management techniques. They also see a shift in consumer demand from goods to services reducing the demand for blue-collar workers, especially the semi-skilled and unskilled, and increasing the demand for white-collar workers, especially professional and technical workers. And they see all this taking place so rapidly that large numbers of jobs are unfilled at the same time that a great many people are out of work. "At the root of the nation's persistent high level of unemployment," two Republican members of Senator Clark's committee wrote in a 1964 committee report, "is the fact that many of the jobless lack the skills that are in demand or do not live where the new jobs are opening up. . . . Right now when we have an unemployment rate exceeding 5 percent many good jobs go begging because we do not have skilled people to fill them. Why is this ironic situation taking place?" The Senators answered this rhetorical question: "Principally, it is due to technological changes which have altered the character of work."

The real question, however, is not whether the structure of employment is changing—after all, the work of the mind has been replacing the work of the hands for a century or more—but how rapidly the change is proceeding. In the opinion of a good many structuralists, the disjuncture between the demand for labor and its supply is so great, and is widening so rapidly, that it will prevent the United States from reaching full employment at *any* level of demand. The demand for highly educated workers is rising and that for the relatively uneducated is falling at such a rapid rate (so the argument goes) that severe shortages of professional, technical, and highly skilled workers would stop the growth of output long before those at the lower end of the education/skill spectrum could be put to work.

But there are good reasons for believing this argument stems from a misunderstanding of the changes that have occurred over the last decade. To be sure, the argument was supported by some impressive-looking evidence. The statistics on output and employment, for example, indicated that there had been a sharp acceleration in two deeply rooted long-term trends: the tendency for labor to shift from the production of goods to the production of services; and in the goods sector itself, the tendency for employers to replace "production workers" (most of whom are semiskilled or unskilled) with "nonproduction workers"—i.e., professional, technical, supervisory, and clerical personnel. Between the first quarter of 1956 and the first quarter of 1961, in manufacturing, 1,700,000 production-worker jobs were eliminated and 500,000 nonproduction workers were added. Thus it seemed plausible to ascribe the sudden shortage of engineers, scientists, and technicians and the huge glut of semiskilled and unskilled production workers to some fundamental alteration in technology and in the structure of the economy.

Plausible as it seemed, the explanation was wrong. The occupational changes of the last decade *were* abnormally large, but the primary cause was not rooted deeply in any new technology or irreversible shift in the structure of consumer demand; instead, the causes were a number of temporary economic and political changes, some of which have run their course while others have already been reversed. Technological change accounts for a surprisingly small proportion of the shifts that have occurred since 1950 in the occupational mix of the labor force. As the previous chapter suggested, confusion about these occupational changes arose out of a historical accident: the development of the computer, which heightened people's awareness of the awesomeness of modern technology, happened to coincide with a slowdown in the rate of economic growth in the late 1950s; at the same time, blue-collar workers were hard hit by the radical post-Korean and post-Sputnik shifts in defense procurement, when the mass production of guns, tanks, trucks, and planes gave way to the "custom" production of missiles and electronic equipment and the sophisticated gadgetry used in exploration of outer space.

Our semiskilled forecasters

Now the shifts in defense procurement have run their course, and the slowdown of the economy has been firmly reversed; but public opinion has not yet caught up to the implications of these facts for the labor market. This chapter will argue that the occupational shifts of the next decade may be less rapid and radical than those of the last. In particular, employment opportunities for blue-collar (especially semiskilled) workers appear to be a lot brighter over the long term than most of the current literature suggests—and also brighter than the recent unemployment rates might lead one to expect. And although employment of highly educated professional and technical workers is bound to keep right on increasing rapidly, the rate of increase may be slower, and the shortages a good deal less acute, than most current forecasts of the labor market seem to indicate.

Those who argue that new structural distortions in the economy are the sole or primary cause of unemployment are saying, in effect, that there are as many unfilled jobs as there are people out of work. Many structuralists assert this explicitly; some have even put the number of vacancies at four million to six million. Others are more cautious: they say that the number of unfilled jobs *now* is uncertain but predict that any increase in aggregate demand would create a vast number of vacancies. They reason that companies would be unable to find employees with the necessary education or skill; hence they could not expand output to meet the rising demand, and inflation rather than full employment would result from it. In any case, all structuralists assume that the number of unfilled jobs has increased substantially over the last decade.

Unfortunately, the Bureau of Labor Statistics does not have any statistics on the number of unfilled jobs (it is now testing some new techniques that will enable it to publish such data). However, the National Industrial Conference Board does publish an index of the volume of help-wanted ads in a number of major cities, and it provides an indirect measure of changes in the number of vacant jobs; at the end of 1964 the index suggested that, if anything, there were *fewer* vacant jobs now than ten years earlier. Field research by *Fortune* also indicated that most of the talk about unfilled jobs was overdone (see also Chapter 7). In the spring of 1964, for example, a trade paper reported that Inland Steel was suffering from a "severe shortage of qualified personnel," as a result of which it was unable to hire all the men it needed for such jobs as riggers, welders, instrument servicemen, and truck drivers. But Inland's vice president for industrial and public relations, William G. Caples, called the report highly exaggerated. "Can you call 284 vacancies in a company of 20,000 people a shortage?" he asked a *Fortune* reporter.

The businessmen *Fortune* talked to did complain about a shortage of educated and trained personnel, all right. But in almost every instance it developed that their firms had as many people in these categories as they were prepared to hire. Quite often, what executives meant in talking about a shortage was that they had difficulty attracting the kind of people they wanted at the rate they felt able to pay; a "shortage" of telephone operators in Washington, D.C., for example, would almost certainly disappear if the telephone company could meet the federal government's clerical salary scale. In a great many other instances, talk of a shortage meant that demand for a particular skill—for example, computer programing—was increasing very rapidly, *not* that firms had fewer programers than they needed at the moment. Sometimes complaints of a shortage simply reflected the fact that the demand for brilliance and creativity *always* exceeds the supply.

The structuralists' concern about unfilled jobs flows from their view of major changes in the workaday world. Some of the changes *are* impressive: since 1950, white-collar employment has increased twice as fast as total employment, and the number of what the Census Bureau calls "professional, technical, and kindred workers" (the category includes engineers, scientists, and doctors, for example) has gone up almost five times as fast. As a result, white-collar workers now compose 44 percent of total employment, compared to 37.5 percent in 1950; the ratio of professional and technical workers is up from 8 to 12 percent of total employment, that of salaried managers from 4 to 6 percent.

But will these sharp gains continue? How rapidly will the "professionalization of the labor force" proceed? To form a judgment, one needs to understand the reasons for what has already occurred. The structuralists say that the reasons are profound changes in technology and in management organization. Specifically, they have assumed that new production processes, and new and more rational techniques of work organization, require the substitution of engineers, scientists, technicians, and managers for production workers in a wide range of industries.

Surprisingly little substitution of this sort has occurred. An exhaustive analysis of occupational changes during the 1950s, conducted by Dr. Joseph N. Froomkin for Columbia University's Bureau of Applied Social Research, indicates that among white-collar workers less than 5 percent of the growth in professional and technical employment, and barely one-third of the growth in clerical employment, can be attributed to the displacement of production workers by nonproduction workers *within* individual industries.* In the case of professional and technical employment, for example, nearly two-thirds of the increase was due to the great expansion of education, medical and hospital care, government services, and religious and other nonprofit institutions.

From tanks to missiles

The demand for teachers, doctors, nurses, social workers, ministers, etc., undoubtedly will continue to grow rapidly for some time to come, although not necessarily at the rate of the last fifteen years. But there already has been a noticeable slowing down in the rate of increase in private industry's demand for professional and technical workers. The shortage of engineers and scientists that evoked so much concern after Sputnik was launched in 1957 (and also evoked so many unflattering comparisons between the United States and the Soviet educational systems) has pretty much vanished. The terrific demand for these kinds of employees had been based, essentially, on the special defense requirements of the mid-1950s—the period that began when the Korean war ended. Indeed, Joseph Froomkin estimates that the change in defense spending, together with our growing effort in space, was responsible for roughly one-quarter of the growth in industry's employment of professional and technical workers during the 1950s.

The defense requirements of the 1950s meant a major shift away from spending on mass-production equipment such as tanks, mortars, trucks, ammunition, and the like. The total dropped from $4.7 billion in fiscal 1953 to $399 million in fiscal 1959. In the same period, however, Defense Department outlays for missiles, electronic equipment, and research and development (including nonmilitary exploration of space) more than doubled—from $3.3 billion in 1953 to $7.1 billion in 1959. These expenditures more than doubled again in the next five years, reaching a peak of $16.0 billion in fiscal 1964.

* Froomkin limited himself to changes between 1950 and 1960 because the decennial censuses provide the only detailed statistics of occupations broken down by industry. Froomkin's analysis is part of a larger study of manpower and productivity now under way at the Bureau of Applied Social Research under the direction of Dr. A. J. Jaffe.

Obviously, this shift in defense procurement meant less demand for production workers and more for technical employees. One Labor Department analysis shows that military-space-electronic plants employ 200 percent more engineers and technicians, but 57 percent *fewer* semiskilled and unskilled workers, than plants producing the same volume of nondefense electronic products. The Labor Department estimates that defense producers as a group employ, proportionately, two-thirds more professional and technical workers but 30 percent fewer semiskilled workers than all United States manufacturing firms. It is scarcely surprising, then, that between 1954 and 1962 the number of engineers employed by industry increased by 276,000; meanwhile, all the engineering schools in the United States graduated only 250,000 engineers, and not all of them went to work for industry. Clearly, industry was able to turn a great many managers, technicians, and craftsmen into engineers. Indeed, about 40 percent of all engineers do not have an engineering degree.

But the shift in defense procurement ran its course; the great wave of increased spending on missiles and on military R. and D. came to a halt in 1964 and early 1965. The results were readily visible in the labor market. "We don't have the same across-the-board volume demand for engineers as in previous years," a North American Aviation spokesman said in the fall of 1964. "There's still a need for certain specialties," the head of a Boston employment firm said, "but it's not the booming, blooming market of a few years ago. It's a far cry from the days when an engineer would be hired first and then the boss would decide what to do with him."

And it is doubtful that *non*defense research and development will take up the slack in this part of the labor market. Although private industry performs three-quarters of all the R. and D. in the United States, it pays for only a third, and industry-financed research has been growing only half as rapidly as government-financed R. and D. Moreover, a good many corporation heads are having skeptical second thoughts about the value they receive for their research dollars. Few companies, if any, are actually cutting back; but many have decided, for the moment, at least, to stabilize the ratio of R. and D. outlays to sales.

Looking into the future, employers of engineers have scaled

down their estimates of requirements. Some 543 corporations and government agencies, employing 40 percent of all degree-holding engineers, were surveyed in 1964 by the Engineering Manpower Commission of the Engineers Joint Council, a body representing virtually all the professional engineering societies. These companies and agencies projected only a 26 percent increase in their employment of engineers over the next decade. (Two years earlier they had been expecting a 45 percent increase.) There is good reason to believe, therefore, that the increase in professional and technical employment over the next five or ten years will be slower than it has been in the past decade—or than many forecasts of the future still suggest.*

Singing the blues

At the same time the demand for blue-collar and other unskilled and semiskilled workers is likely to be a lot firmer than the structuralist view suggests. As Chapter 1 pointed out, the question is not whether technology is changing—clearly, it is—or even whether such change displaces substantial numbers of workers. Technological innovation is always reducing the number of workers needed in a particular process and altering the kinds of skills required, and the change is always painful to the people involved. The real question posed by the structuralist view is whether displacement of semiskilled and unskilled workers is occurring at a substantially faster rate than in the past—at a rate so fast, in fact, as to create unemployment by making large numbers of people with little education or relatively modest skills unemployable. The answer, quite simply, is that it is not.

The structuralists make a good deal of the fact that the ratio of production workers to total manufacturing employment is a good deal lower now than it was in the early postwar period. Some decline in the proportion of manufacturing production workers did occur in the early postwar period, but this merely restored the ratio that had prevailed all through the 1920s and 1930s. (During the war, of course, the ratio had risen as every available person was

* The increase in defense spending in connection with the war in Vietnam may push up demand for engineers once again. It already has pushed up demand for blue-collar workers.

put to work on the factory floor.) The old ratio held between 1951 and 1953, when a new decline did set in. But *that* decline came to a halt in 1961, and the proportion of manufacturing workers in production jobs has been stable since then; the absolute number of production workers has increased by over one million since 1961. Thus the period in which the proportion of production workers declined may be viewed most simply as an exceptional eight years. Employment of manufacturing production workers was hard hit by the relative stagnation of industry in that period—in particular, by the decline in sales of cars and other consumer durables after 1955 and by the collapse of the capital-goods market after 1957. Nonproduction workers were less affected because firms are much slower to lay off managers, engineers, salesmen, clerks, and foremen.

To say this, of course, does not exhaust the argument, for a good many of the structuralists regard that economic slowdown during the middle and late 1950s not as exceptional, but as the harbinger of profound changes. In their view the slowdown occurred because of what Professor Killingsworth calls "the maturing of the mass-consumption society." Consumers, the argument goes, are relatively sated with cars, appliances, houses, and other goods; as a result, consumer demand is shifting away from goods (for which blue-collar workers are needed) and toward services, which require great numbers of professional workers.

But it seems unreasonable to view the slowdown in the rate of economic growth during the late 1950s as the beginning of secular stagnation; it may also be taken as a happy substitute for the crash that followed the boom after other wars. In retrospect, *some* slowdown in the rate of economic growth was inevitable after 1953. The great boom of 1947–53 had been generated by the backlogs of demand for both consumer and capital goods built up during the preceding fifteen years, as well as by the great postwar surge in marriages, household formation, and births. The boom had been fueled by the enormous liquidity of consumers and corporations during and just after World War II, when incomes and profits were high but few goods were available for purchase. By 1955 or 1956, this liquidity had been sopped up, and both consumers and corporations were heavily in debt. At the same time the backlogs of demand had been satisfied; future increases in

Chart 3. Employment by Source of Demand

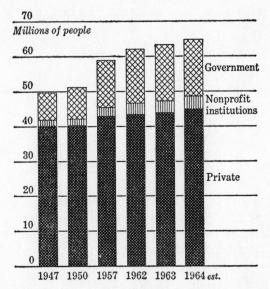

Chronic pessimists about the economy argue that private demand has become too weak to create new jobs. After a sharp increase in 1950–57, it accounted for only a few new jobs (400,000 out of 3,100,000) in 1957–62. But in the next two years, private demand provided three new jobs in five—1,700,000 of the 2,900,000 net new jobs added. (Those employed by business but producing goods and services for government—e.g., planes, roads—have been included in governmental demand.)

demand would have to be geared more closely to increases in income and population; and the population changes were now working, temporarily, against large increases in demand.

But what might have been a brief slowdown in the rate of economic growth was prolonged by a series of historical accidents. In 1957 excessive monetary restraint by the Federal Reserve, coming on top of a modest reduction in capital spending, produced the most severe recession of the postwar period. The recovery from that recession was then aborted by a 116-day steel strike in 1959 and by a renewal of monetary and fiscal restraint—the most severe of the postwar period. Even the weather conspired against

Chart 4. Employment by Kind of Industry

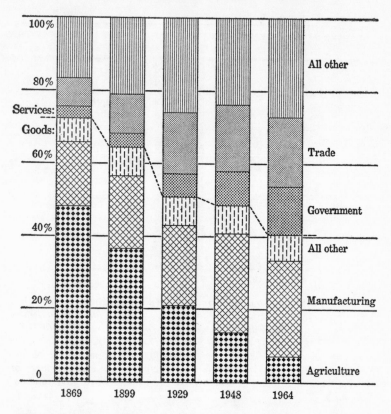

Recent experience also explodes the notion that the shift from goods to services is accelerating. The reduction in goods employment (below dotted line) has been concentrated in agriculture, and that shift, which began a hundred years ago, is slowing down now. The proportion of workers in nonagricultural-goods production has been remarkably stable, edging off only from 35.1 percent in 1948 to 33.4 percent in 1964.

recovery: the snows in the winter of 1960 were the worst in years, choking off some of the increase in consumer spending that materialized after the strike had ended. The whole picture is an example of what the economist Thorstein Veblen used to call a "concatenation of fortuitous circumstances."

As soon as monetary and fiscal restraint was ended, however, the economy turned around and started to expand—a remarkable demonstration of the underlying strength of consumer and business demand. In March 1966, the expansion began its sixth year, making it the longest in the peacetime history of the United States. The expansion has been impressive, not only because of its length, but even more for its strength and depth. Between the first quarter of 1961 and the first quarter of 1966, the gross national product increased by 31 percent, measured in constant dollars; the *increment* has been larger than the entire G.N.P. of Canada. And the growth in our G.N.P. has not been limited to the services sector; output of goods has increased 38 percent. And the capital-goods and consumer-durables industries, which had lagged so badly in the preceding period, have shown the most vigorous expansion of all. Indeed, these markets have grown 50 percent faster in the current boom than they did in 1947–53.

Maturity in 1886

For all the talk about the shift from goods to services, more-over, the fact is that industrial production has grown more rapidly than G.N.P. throughout the postwar period—i.e., by 4.4 percent a year vs. 3.8 percent. The margin has widened sharply since 1961, thanks to the boom in capital goods, cars, and appliances. And there are solid reasons for believing that industrial production will continue to grow at least as rapidly as G.N.P. in the foreseeable future. The proposition that "economic maturity" will dampen demand and so restrict the economy's growth rate has been trotted out in almost every recession, depression, and slowdown for the last eighty years. Back in 1886, for example, the U.S. Commissioner of Labor said that the United States, along with most European countries, had about exhausted the possibility of further economic growth: "The market price of products will continue low, no matter what the cost of production may be. The day of

Chart 5. Net Change in Labor Force by Age Groups

Age groups ■14-19 ▦20-24 ▨25-34 ▥35-54 ⊠55 and over

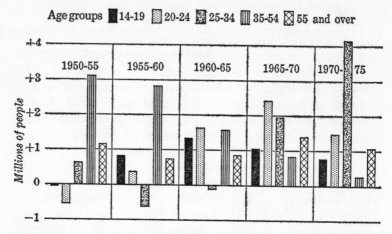

The great teenage boom is ending now. The age structure of the labor force has been changing rapidly. Between 1950 and 1955 the number of teenagers in the labor force declined by 61,000, the number of twenty- to twenty-four-year-olds by 596,000. The baby boom right after World War II began to be felt in 1955–60, when the teenagers increased by 864,000. Teenage entry into the labor market was at flood tide in 1965; the increase came to about 500,000, compared to an 810,000 increase in the preceding four years, and about one million between 1965 and 1970.

large profits is probably past. There may be room for further intensive, but not extensive, development of industry in the present area of civilization."

The fact that pessimism was misplaced in the past, of course, doesn't necessarily prove that it is inappropriate for the present. But there is little basis for the view that Americans are sated with goods and that only modest increases in consumer purchases of goods can be expected. The median household income in the United States in 1964 was $5,696; it is patently absurd to suggest that the 30 million households earning less than that sum would be hard put to find things to buy if their incomes increased. Even at $10,000 a year, a family scarcely has a sybaritic standard of living; and only 19 percent of all households earn that much. At what point, indeed, do people stop "needing" more goods? In

Chart 6. Unemployment Rates by Age Groups

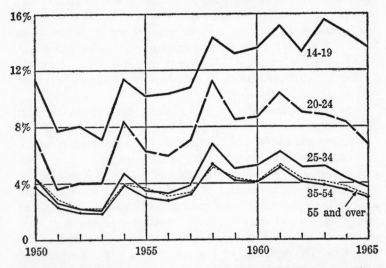

The end of the great teenage boom may help to hold down unemployment. A heavy supply of teenagers is a problem because they have always had a high unemployment rate; they lack job skills and experience, as well as the pressure of family responsibility. (Over half the teenagers in the labor force are also in school.) In 1953, when only 2.9 percent of the labor force was unemployed, the teenage rate was 7.1 percent—two and a half times as high. The margin has widened as the number of teenagers mushroomed; in 1965 their unemployment rate (13.6 percent) was three times the over-all rate.

1948 *Fortune* studied the spending habits of a group of executives earning $25,000 a year or more—the equivalent of $32,000 today—and found that none of them were able to live within their incomes; their expenditures exceeded income by an average of $1,870.25 a year. There is no evidence that this privileged group—1 percent of all households—is any more solvent today. If families earning upwards of $30,000 a year are not yet sated, there is reason to assume that consumer markets can keep growing in line with income for quite some time to come.

Another good reason for expecting consumer sales to hold up is that demographic factors will be working to expand them—especially sales of housing and durable goods. The youngsters born during the huge baby boom of World War II and the early postwar years are beginning to reach maturity: the population aged twenty to twenty-nine—which accounts for the vast majority of marriages and household formations—will increase by about 25 percent in the next five years. (The number reaching twenty-one will take a sudden, discrete jump of 35 percent in 1967–68.) Hence the number of marriages is likely to run above two million a year until well into the 1970s.

Consumer expenditures might be stimulated, too, by the fact that the huge stock of durables purchased during the mid-1950s is wearing out and will have to be replaced. The normal annual scrappage rate for automobiles, for example, has risen by more than one million cars since 1955—from four million to 5,500,000. For the first time since the end of World War II, in fact, a big upsurge in replacement requirements will coincide with a big upsurge in demand stemming from population growth. The conjuncture cannot, of course, guarantee renewed expansion in the late 1960s. The argument here is not that industrial markets *will* expand at a rapid rate, but that they *can,* and that the case for a forecast of stagnation is weak.

The need for service

The likeliest prospect, then, is a growing demand for manufacturing production workers. The strongest demand of all will be felt by the skilled workers, the weakest by the unskilled. This differen- explains why unskilled laborers now represent less than 10 percent of the manufacturing production-worker total. For the semiskilled and skilled workers who make up the great bulk of the production-worker force, technological innovation tends to change the content of the job, but not the level of skill required.

In any case, half or more of all blue-collar workers are employed *outside* manufacturing—a point many structuralists seem to forget. Two million of the three million unskilled laborers work in other parts of the economy; and while the total number of laborers is declining, employment is increasing rapidly in a number of unskilled occupations. (The number of gardeners and ground- tial is nothing new; it has been manifest for half a century, and keepers went up 40 percent between 1950 and 1960.) More than a third of the semiskilled blue-collar workers are employed outside manufacturing—e.g., truck drivers, bus drivers. And two-thirds of the nearly nine million skilled craftsmen work in nonmanufacturing industries—two million of them in construction and nearly one million in trade.

More important, the structuralists generally ignore the very rapidly expanding demand for what the Census Bureau calls "service workers." Employment of service workers, who are not included in the blue-collar figures, has increased more than twice as fast as total employment in the last fifteen years. With few exceptions, service jobs do not require very much education or training. On the contrary, they tend to be relatively menial and unskilled—e.g., charwomen (whose number increased over 50 percent during the 1950s), cooks, countermen, waiters, hospital attendants. On every forecast, the number of service workers is expected to grow faster than total employment into the indefinite future. All in all, therefore, the United States has a long way to go before people who do not have a high school education can be deemed unemployable.

How much dynamite?

Why did the United States take so long to achieve full employment?

The explanation lies in the large pool of unemployment that existed when the boom began, and in the above-average gains in the size of the labor force after the boom got under way. To have brought the unemployment rate down to 4 percent in the last quarter of 1964, instead of the 5 percent average that prevailed, would have required the G.N.P. to grow by 5.2 percent a year since 1961, instead of the actual 4.9 percent.

In some ways, the unemployment situation in 1964–65 was less serious than the over-all figures suggest. From the standpoint of the human costs that are involved, the composition of unemployment may be as important as its over-all level. Married men, for example, represent the most important group within the labor force, since they provide the major sources of income for households. For this group, unemployment in the last quarter of 1964 averaged 2.6 percent—about half the rate for the entire labor force, and about the same as this group experienced in 1955–57, when the labor force was at, or close to, full employment. (By the fourth quarter of 1965, the rate was down to 2.0 percent.)

Young people, on the other hand, make up a disproportionately large part of the unemployed. In 1964, people between the ages of fourteen and twenty-four represented less than 20 percent of the labor force, but more than 40 percent of the unemployed. Teen-agers by themselves are the worst off: they represented 8 percent of the labor force in 1964 but *22 percent* of the unemployed. Youth unemployment constitutes a serious and special national problem; it will be discussed in detail in the next chapter. But the problem posed by out-of-work youth is a good deal less serious, and a good deal more manageable, than, say, the situation of the 1930s, when married men found it as difficult as youngsters to land or hold jobs. And while unemployment touches the lives of an astonishingly large proportion of the labor force—about 14 million separate individuals were out of work at one time or another in 1964—surprisingly few people remain unemployed for very long periods. Out of the 3,700,000 unemployed in the last quarter of 1964, fewer than 920,000 had been out of work for more than fourteen weeks, fewer than 445,000 for more than six months. (By the fourth quarter of 1965, these totals were down to 673,000 and 321,000, resectively.)

Over the long term, the level of unemployment will depend, as it always has, primarily on whether the economy grows fast enough to absorb the manpower made available by increases in the labor force together with rising man-hour productivity. In all probability, productivity will grow somewhat faster than its average for the entire postwar period, although less rapidly than in the 1960–65 period. The labor force will also grow more rapidly than it has in the past, although some of *this* growth may be siphoned off by a reduction in the work week or, more likely, a reduction in the work year through longer vacations. To maintain full employment, therefore, the economy will have to grow more rapidly than in the past. There is nothing in the structure of the labor market to prevent that from happening.

3

What Hit the Teenagers?

IN THE UNITED STATES, Eric Larrabee has remarked, childhood "is not only admired; it is looked upon as a national asset, somewhat on a par with the Declaration of Independence or the Mississippi River." But while childhood is regarded as a national asset, adolescence seems more and more to be regarded as a national problem, like traffic congestion, water pollution, or slums. Specifically, the problem associated with teenagers is unemployment. Dr. James B. Conant, who helped direct national attention to the problem, has described it as "social dynamite"; President Kennedy called it "one of the most expensive and explosive social and economic problems now facing this country"; and Lyndon Johnson has given expansion of teenage employment top priority on the road to the Great Society. For teenagers, who represented just 8 percent of the labor force in 1964, accounted for 22 percent of total unemployment and about 35 percent of the *increase* in unemployment since the middle 1950s. All told, nearly 850,000 teenagers—14 percent of those in the labor force—were looking for work at the end of 1964; another 300,000 teenage boys were for various reasons, neither in school nor in the labor force. (Some were waiting to go into the Army, some were delinquents, some were unable to work, and some were just drifting.)

There is a certain irony, of course, in the fact that providing more jobs for teenagers has become a major concern of statesmen and of social reformers; during most of this century and part of the last, reformers' zeal was devoted to the *elimination* of child labor. In 1904 the National Child Labor Committee was organized to further that cause. In 1959, after voting down several suggestions that the organization be dissolved, since its original goal had long since been achieved, the trustees instead established the National Committee on Employment of Youth. *Its* objective is "to create greater job opportunities for America's youth." At first, the new committee (technically, a division of the old) felt the need to persuade people that a shortage of teenage jobs really was a problem. "With all the headlines about delinquency," the committee's publicity director told the readers of the New York *Times,* in a somewhat plaintive letter to the editor," "it is important to remember that this is only one of many juvenile problems . . . teenagers need help in planning for, choosing, and getting suitable jobs . . ."

It didn't require a new organization, however, to bring teenage unemployment to the forefront of public consciousness. The recent increases in the number of teenagers wanting to work have created a labor-market situation without precedent in the last half-century. One would have to go back to around 1900 to find another peacetime period when the teenage labor force was growing so rapidly. But the teenage labor market then was an entirely different proposition. A third of the population was living on the farm, only 15 percent of the high school age youngsters were actually attending school, and fewer than 10 percent of them finished. The great majority went to work after the sixth or eighth grade. In the cities, working-class families depended on the children's earnings to supplement the father's meager wage; and farm families were even more dependent on child labor.

But the growth of free and compulsory education signaled a new trend—and the end of any large expansion of the teenage labor force. Between 1910 and 1940 the proportion of fourteen-to-seventeen-year-olds attending high school went up from 15 percent to more than 70 percent; the proportion graduating from high school went up from under 10 percent to over 50 percent. This change was accompanied (and to a considerable degree caused) by the enormous migration of Americans from the farm, where teenage labor was particularly valuable, to the city. In 1910 teenagers had been about 15 percent of the labor force; by 1940 they were 7.5 percent of it.

This long-run contraction of teenage employment was temporarily reversed during World War II, when every available hand was put to work. But it resumed as soon as the war ended; between 1947 and 1955 the number of teenagers in the labor force declined by 200,000 as the teenage "participation rate"—i.e., the proportion who were either at work or looking for work—continued to fall.

The participation rate is still declining, as the proportion of teenagers completing high school and attending college continues to rise. But the teenage population has been growing so rapidly that this declining percentage now represents a growing number. Between 1955 and 1960 the teenage labor force increased by 900,000, and it grew almost as much again between 1960 and 1964. It is now about six and a half million.*

A search for something

Adolescence, as Professor Edgar Z. Friedenberg of the University of California has defined it, "is the period during which a young person learns who he is, and what he really feels." In the phrase of psychiatrist Erik H. Erikson, of Harvard, it is "the search for something and somebody to be true to." It is difficult for

---

* Some of the figures used in this article differ from those published by the Bureau of Labor Statistics. *Fortune*'s figures, based on unpublished BLS data, are "school-year averages"; the published BLS statistics are annual averages. Since the teenage labor force runs 45 percent higher during the summer months than during the school year, an annual average overstates (by 650,000) the number of youngsters who are normally in the labor force.

More important, the annual averages substantially understate the number of teenagers who are students: during the summer months BLS classifies as students only those actually attending summer school. Thus students who go away to camp during the summer, or travel with their parents, or just loaf, are statistically indistinguishable from the "dropouts." In 1964, for example, the published figures (averaging all twelve months) show a rather frightening total of 1,045,000 teenage boys who were neither in school nor in the labor force. For the nine months of the school year, however, there were 70 percent fewer, i.e., 300,000.

a youngster to learn who he is under the best of circumstances. It is even harder if he is unemployed, for unemployment can make the most secure man feel useless and unwanted. It is particularly hard for an unemployed adolescent to feel true to the society he lives in if he has an impoverished background. Indeed, the slum youngster's unemployment seems only to confirm his well-grounded suspicion that he can't "make it"—that decent jobs are not available to young people of his color, or his nationality, or his social class. The gates of life seem to clang shut when he is still at a remarkably early age.

Thus the concern now being expressed about teenage unemployment is amply justified. But the explanations of how the problem has come about, and what it portends, are inadequate. In the most common view, a high level of teenage unemployment is a symptom of far-reaching technological and economic changes. Technological change is said to be destroying unskilled jobs, most especially the traditional "entry jobs" through which teenagers used to make their way into the labor force—i.e., jobs that could be filled by youngsters with little education and no particular skill or training, but that might lead to more skilled and better-paying jobs later on. Eli E. Cohen, executive secretary of the National Committee on Employment of Youth, has estimated that some 250,000 "entry jobs" a year are disappearing as a result of technological change. Meanwhile—the argument continues—new technology is constantly increasing the educational requirements of jobs. "The machine," Secretary of Labor Willard Wirtz contends, "now has a high school education in the sense that it can do most jobs that a high school graduate can do, so machines will get the jobs because they work for less than a living wage. A person needs fourteen years of education to compete with machines."

In short, Wirtz, Cohen, and others see the teenage unemployment problems as rooted in the dwindling opportunities for the uneducated and untrained. In contrast to the 1920s or 1930s, they also believe, formal education and training have become young people's only reliable means of entry into the world of work. That is why Wirtz has proposed that an additional two years of school attendance be made compulsory. "Boys and girls simply have to be trained to fit into an economy which no longer includes the unskilled work they could get before. Anybody who drops out of school may very well be committing economic suicide." In a 1963 address Wirtz recalled that thirty years previously, when he taught high school literature and grammar, very little of *Macbeth* or English syntax got through to the students. "But it didn't matter," he went on, for this was "a town where most of the boys were going into the boiler works, and if the girls didn't get married, they would probably get work at the glove factory." (The town, which Wirtz did not name, was Kewanee, Illinois.)

Why can't Johnny work?

Plausible as it sounds, this diagnosis both oversimplifies and overcomplicates the current situation, and contrasts it with a past that never was. In general, as the first two chapters demonstrated, it is simply not true that new technology is eliminating the demand for relatively unskilled or poorly educated blue-collar workers; nor is technology increasing the demand for people with a great deal of education and professional or technical training as rapidly as Wirtz suggests. In particular, the much-discussed disappearance of "entry jobs" is a myth, based upon some fanciful reconstruction of the kinds of jobs teenagers used to get, and how they used to get them. Actually, those "entry jobs" that have been disappearing— e.g., bowling-alley pinboy, Western Union messenger, elevator operator—have typically been dead-end jobs, not jobs that led to something. And meanwhile a great many new jobs that teenagers can fill have been created, especially in trade and service industries.

Most important of all, the official diagnosis blurs the real problem about the dropouts. The problem is indeed a critical one for our society; but it is not, we shall see below, simply a matter of persuading potential dropouts to stay in school.

Why, then, *are* there so many unemployed teenagers? The answer, stripped to its essentials, is that the sudden expansion of the teenage population happened to coincide with the slowdown in the economy between 1957 and 1961. Teenagers had the bad luck to begin pouring into the labor force at a time when there was an oversupply of adult workers. Given a choice between experienced or, in any case, comparatively stable adults and inexperienced and relatively unstable teenagers, employers naturally hired the adults.

Typically, the adults in question were women; working wives

often seek—and get—the kind of unskilled and part-time jobs that are most suitable for teenagers. To a degree that has not generally been appreciated, teenagers have been competing for jobs with their mothers. One of the major difficulties about finding jobs for teenagers has been the enormous, and completely unanticipated, increase in the proportion of married women who are in the labor force: from 20 percent in 1947 to 26 percent in 1953 and 34 percent in 1964. Had their participation rate stayed at the 1947 level, there would have been nearly six million fewer women working in 1964.

Why the standards are up

Not surprisingly, the labor surplus led to a stiffening of hiring standards all along the line. Thus adults without any previous work experience—for example, married women looking for part-time jobs while their children are in school—also had difficulty finding jobs; when there is a choice, employers prefer an experienced to an inexperienced adult. *People seeking their first jobs constitute twice as large a proportion of the unemployed today as they did a decade ago.*

A distinction is in order at this point. Employers have raised the educational requirements for new employees—but not necessarily because the technical requirements of the jobs have changed. A great many employers have made a high school diploma a prerequisite for employment simply as a screening device, to cut down the number of people who have to be interviewed or to ensure "a better class of workers." To some degree, publicity campaigns to persuade youngsters to stay in school, or to return if they've already dropped out, may make it harder for those who do drop out to find a job; if enough people are persuaded that dropouts are unemployable, they will insist on hiring only high school graduates (or teenagers clearly determined to finish school) even for dead-end jobs.

Some companies are now discovering that they have overdone this upgrading. They are even learning that for some jobs the unambitious or not-too-bright dropout may be preferable to the high school graduate. In staffing two plants, for example, Ford hired many young high school graduates, expecting that this would raise productivity. Instead, the policy lowered productivity and increased absenteeism; the new workers tended to find the assembly line oppressive. In any case, Ford has substituted a literacy test administered by the United States Employment Service for formal credentials like high school diplomas.

Life on the margin

Teenage unemployment has been too high, not because the relatively unskilled and the poorly educated are unemployable, but because the aggregate demand for labor has been weak—which is to say, because the economy has not grown rapidly enough. Professor Stanley Lebergott of Wesleyan University, a profound academic student of the labor force, is one of the few who have argued persuasively against the notion that the unemployed are victims of under-education. This notion, he says, "misapprehends at least one fundamental characteristic of the unemployed"—the fact that they "are marginal in the existing state of offer and demand in the labor market. If all workers in the labor force had their education improved," Lebergott argues, "some would still be marginal," but "their marginality would then appear to be associated with some other simple single characteristic."

To be sure, the educational level of the entire labor force (i.e., including the unemployed) is rising rapidly; the median number of years of schooling of labor-force members aged eighteen to sixty-four went from 9.1 in 1940 to 11.1 in 1952 and 12.2 in 1964, and the proportion of workers with a high school education or better rose from 32 percent in 1940 and 44 percent in 1952 to 57 percent in 1964. But this change is the result of a great many things having nothing whatever to do with the amount of education people need for the job. The educational attainment of the labor force has risen because of the shift of population from rural to urban areas (a much larger proportion of youngsters finish high school in urban areas); the expansion of facilities for public education throughout the country; the rise in average income (which enables young people to say in school longer); and a radical change in public attitudes toward education. Thus even the average laborer, household domestic, or service worker—as well as the craftsman, technician, or clerk—has more education than he had ten years ago.

In any case, there is no evidence of any decline in the number of "entry jobs." A detailed manpower survey by the New York State Department of Labor, for example, revealed that approximately two-thirds of all the jobs in existence in that state involve such simple skills that they can be—and are—learned in a few days, weeks, or at most months of on-the-job training. And the fact is that nearly half the Americans holding jobs today did not finish high school. Indeed, studies by Dr. A. J. Jaffe of Columbia University's Bureau of Applied Social Research indicate that even in industries experiencing the most rapid technological change and the highest rate of productivity growth half or more of the male production workers did not finish high school, i.e., they are "dropouts."

It is also a fact that in 1962, when output expanded by 6.6 percent, and in 1964, when output increased by 5.0 percent, and again in 1965, when output went up by 5.4 percent, the economy was able to provide enough jobs to offset the entire increase in the teenage labor force. Indeed, teenagers accounted for 17 percent of the increase in employment in 1962 and in 1964, and no less than 30 percent in 1965. In 1963, on the other hand, when the growth rate slowed down to 3.8 percent, the number of jobs filled by teenagers actually declined.

The turn to competition

At the same time, the structure of teenage employment has changed substantially in the last thirty years or so, as the chart on page 54 demonstrates.* The most striking change is the decline

* The chart is based on data developed for *Fortune* by Alan Greenspan of Townsend-Greenspan & Co. from the decennial censuses for 1930 and 1960. The decennial censuses were used because only they provide the kind of detailed data necessary for such an analysis; 1930 was chosen as the base year because it is about the closest one can come to a "normal" pre-World War II year. The figures are necessarily imprecise because the Census Bureau used different definitions and different techniques of enumeration in the two years; however, the orders of magnitude may be considered reliable.

of 900,000 in the number of teenage agricultural workers. One-third of the teenage workers were on the farm in 1930, most of them classified as "unpaid family workers"—hence outside the operation of the competitive labor market; by 1960 the ratio was down to 10 percent. The change is even greater for teenage boys: 50 percent of the fourteen-to-seventeen-year-old boys, and 30 percent of the eighteen-to-nineteen-year-olds, were farm laborers in 1930. Most of the boys, in short, did not go directly into the boiler works when they abandoned *Macbeth;* only 27 percent of the teenage workers in 1930, in fact, were employed in manufacturing industries.

For all the talk about the disappearing "entry jobs," the number of unskilled and semiskilled teenage jobs outside of agriculture has increased twice as fast as the teenage population. Between 1930 and 1960 the number of teenage boys who were laborers and semiskilled blue-collar workers increased by 115,000, or 12 percent. It is true that teenage employment in manufacturing declined in these years; and Secretary Wirtz is right in suggesting that not many boys go into the boiler works nowadays. But plenty of them do go to work in the local supermarket, gas station, or parking lot. Or they become ushers, hospital attendants, busboys, or waiters; the number of such teenage "service workers" went up by 200,000, a threefold increase since 1930. The number of "sales workers" also increased by 200,000, but about three-quarters of that increase represents an expansion in the number of newspaper delivery boys.

Some traditional teenage jobs have virtually disappeared, of course. But they were never very important: there were just 5,000 to 6,000 male teenage elevator operators in 1930 (there are fewer than 2,000 now), and the number of teenage Western Union messengers never exceeded 13,000, compared to 2,500 or thereabouts now. And despite the displacement of bowling-alley pinboys by automatic pinsetting machines, more teenage boys work in bowling alleys today than in 1930—e.g., as cashiers, porters, and "pin-chasers" (unjamming jammed automatic pinsetters).

Many of the jobs teenagers hold—perhaps even the majority—are essentially dead-end jobs. They *always* were; much of the current discussion about youth employment is based on nostalgia for a past that never existed—on what might be called "the

Chart 7. Net Change in Number of Teenage Workers 1930–60

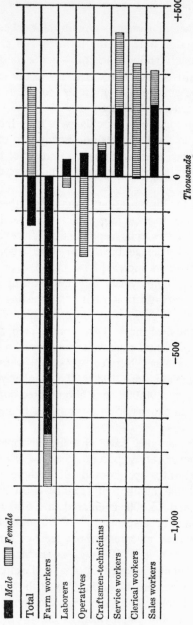

The teenage unemployment crisis has not arisen only because there are more teenagers than ever. Actually, there are not many more in the labor force than there were in 1930. What has changed is that most are now in the competitive labor market, whereas in 1930 a large proportion were "unpaid family workers"—typically helping around the farm. The number of teenage farm workers declined by 900,000 between 1930 and 1960. Meanwhile, the number of nonfarm workers increased by 1,020,000 or one-third. The biggest increase, evenly divided between boys and girls, was in the form of 420,000 more "service workers," e.g., waiters and waitresses, hospital attendants.

sweatshops were fun" view of the case. Thus the U.S. Employment Service officially laments the fact that "the time has passed when a young worker can begin an occupation with assurance that he has entered a lifetime vocation." Whenever that time was, it is not within the memory of anyone now alive.

Half or more of the teenagers in the labor market, moreover, have no particular desire to begin "a lifetime vocation"; they simply want a job that won't interfere too much with their studies. Some 3,200,000 teenagers—55 percent of those in the labor force—are also students, most of them holding or looking for jobs after school or during summer vacations. *All the increase in the teenage labor force in recent years—and all the increase in teenage unemployment—has occurred among teenagers attending school.*

Table 1. The School-Age Population, 1964
(*school-year averages, in thousands*)

Age	14–17	18–19	20–21	22–24
Total	*13,864*	*5,164*	*5,181*	*6,831*
NOT IN SCHOOL				
In labor force	593	2,116	2,925	4,425
Employed	474	1,816	2,635	4,137
Unemployed	119	300	290	288
Not in labor force	619	771	1,137	1,909
TOTAL	1,212	2,887	4,062	6,334
IN SCHOOL				
In labor force	2,515	655	336	168
Employed	2,203	550	290	142
Unemployed	312	105	a	a
Not in labor force	10,137	1,622	783	329
TOTAL	12,652	2,277	1,119	497

a Less than 100,000.

It is natural to think of teenagers as being either in school or at work, but many are both. Among fourteen- to seventeen-year-olds, for example, 91 percent, or 12,652,000, were in school; 2,203,000 of these were also working (mostly part time) and 312,000 were looking for work. Of the 1,212,000 out-of-school fourteen- to seventeen-year-olds, 474,000 were working and 119,000 were unemployed. In the ages between twenty and twenty-four, almost a third of those in school were in the labor force. Those not in school or the labor force are predominantly girls. (Figures refer to the civilian population only.)

Between 1962 and early 1965, the number of students in the labor force went up by 450,000, or 17 percent. In the same period the number of unemployed students increased by 150,000, or 54 percent. More than half the unemployed teenage boys are now students.

The student workers represent an extraordinary new phenomenon. "This youthful work economy," the sociologist Reuel Denney of the University of Hawaii, has written, "is not, by and large, vocationally directed, even though it may serve as a way of trying out possible occupations. It is rather a form of paid sociability combined with study, an existence in which the student-waiter brings some of the campus to the resort and uses the pool after hours."

Not every student works as a waiter or a lifeguard in a summer resort, of course; many depend on year-round jobs to keep them in school. But for most, the earnings from a job are only one of several sources of income: parental support, private scholarships, public scholarships, and wages are all mingled together. Working after school or during vacations is no longer the mark of respectable poverty; on the contrary, students from middle-income families are more likely to be in the labor force than students from low-income families—perhaps because it is easier for the former to find jobs.

The real teenage employment problem involves the *out*-of-school youngsters. Contrary to the general impression, the out-of-school teenage labor force has not been growing in the last several years. The number of unemployed out-of-school teenage boys has actually declined slightly—from 243,000 in 1962 to 223,000 in 1964. It is these boys, three-fifths of them dropouts—plus 300,000 more, one-third to one-half of whom could have been in the labor force but weren't—who constitute what Wirtz calls the "outlaw pack."* Many of them appear to be unemployable: they are—or seem to be—uninterested in working, unwilling or unable to adjust to the routine and discipline of a job, and generally

---

* Some economists define "the youth employment problem" as involving sixteen- to twenty-one-year-olds. In this age group there were, in 1964, 386,000 unemployed out-of-school males and 309,000 out of school and out of the labor force; perhaps 100,000 to 150,000 could be in the labor force.

apathetic, sullen, or hostile. Others seem willing enough to work, but have trouble following any task through to completion.

It is understandable that adults view these nonworking teenagers with deep misgivings, and that they are confounded by the story Wirtz tells of asking an unemployed Harlem teenager whether he was looking for a job, and the youngster's replying, "Why?" To an adult, the answer seems obvious: men work because they have to. And thirty or forty years ago teenagers worked for the same reason—because of economic necessity, their own or their parents'. The children's earnings were depended upon to supplement the father's; the mother stayed home to raise the children. It was simply taken for granted that youngsters went to work when they left school; that was, in fact, why they left.

Why won't Johnny work?

Today's teenagers, even those in slums, are in a quite different situation. If the family is intact, it is now the mother who is supplementing the father's wage. If the family is not intact the Welfare Department or the federal Aid to Dependent Children program provides the supplement.

Teenagers also lack the psychological pressures that make the great majority of adult men prefer work to idleness. In adult society, as Professor David Riesman has put it, "holding down a job is necessary to a sense of responsible and respectable adulthood." Not only do most working-class men believe that it is a man's duty to "bring home the bacon"; a sizable minority, Riesman argues, "believe that marriage is important because it provides a man with a family for whom he may work"—a paradoxical reversal of the comic-strip stereotype of male resentment at having been trapped by marriage into a life of servitude.

But these social and cultural pressures to work don't operate very effectively in teenage society; holding down a job is not necessarily a source of status, as in adult society, nor is unemployment a source of shame. On the contrary, in at least some city slums, teenage society displays a certain disdain for legitimate work. The kinds of menial jobs that are available are regarded as "slaving"; status and prestige attach, rather, to "the tough guy" who affects a show of bravado or to "the hustler" who earns his living through petty criminality—e.g., as a runner for a numbers game.

And to the extent that work *is* a value to teenagers, the kind of work that is valued may not be the kind that is available—and certainly not the kind that leads to middle-class status. There is, in lower-class culture, a respect for manual or outdoor labor, especially labor having to do with *things,* and a corresponding disdain for many white-collar and service jobs; more precisely, there is a fear that holding such a job may diminish the teenager's virility. "We're outdoor types"; "we like to fiddle with engines," young men interviewed by *Fortune* remarked, in explaining why they were reluctant to go back to school to qualify for white-collar jobs. "Only finks do I.B.M."

But if there is a disdain for white-collar work, so is there, quite often, a resentment of unskilled or semiskilled service jobs as too servile or degrading. Americans, and particularly young Americans, balk at accepting the role implied or required in such jobs as waiter, hospital attendant, household domestic; we do not have the British tradition of service without servility. Yet these jobs—not those for which a high school diploma is really necessary—are the ones for which there is an unfilled and rapidly growing demand. (On the Labor Department's own calculations, the supply of high school graduates over the next ten years will be "adequate to meet the demand for workers with this amount of education.")

The problem is compounded by the fact that service jobs tend to be badly paid, as well as low in status. The New Jersey Employment Service had great difficulty finding teenage applicants in Newark for a program to train hospital attendants. Applicants were assured a job if they finished the course. But the job, which was an hour-and-a-quarter bus ride away (weekly commutation: $5.20), paid $50 a week.

The problems, then, are considerable; and yet the teenage dropout is not a hopeless case. One striking characteristic of adolescence is its transiency: what the social workers' blandishments cannot accomplish, the process of aging can, and does. As the youngsters grow up, the same societal pressures that make the rest of us work begin to operate on them, too: they want to get married, have children, or at least move away from home into "pads" of their own. And so the youngsters who were delinquents at sixteen or seventeen turn into law-abiding citizens at twenty or twenty-one; those who seemed unemployable at seventeen or eighteen begin to settle down at nineteen or twenty and look for a steady job.

The process of finding one takes time; finding "the right job," in particular, can be a hit-or-miss affair, since employee and employer are usually brought together by word of mouth. (Only one-quarter of all hirings in the economy involve the use of a public or private employment service.) Hence eighteen- and nineteen-year-old boys change jobs more than twice as often as fourteen- to seventeen-year-olds. Job changes reach a peak among the twenty- to twenty-four-year-olds, but then drop abruptly, as family responsibilities and seniority rights stabilize employment. Indeed, among eighteen-and nineteen-year-old married men, the unemployment rate in 1964 was 6.6 percent; for single men the same age it was 15.3 percent; and among twenty- to twenty-four-year-olds the unemployment rate for married men was only 4.3 percent, compared to 11.9 percent for single men.

None of this is intended to suggest that the aging process is a satisfactory solution to the teenage unemployment problem. Even among twenty- to twenty-one-year-old men, the unemployment rate for dropouts runs to 18 percent, compared to 9 percent for high school graduates. More important, when the dropouts find work, as most ultimately do, they are likely to be restricted to mean, dirty, badly paid jobs.

But persuading the dropouts to return to school, or requiring potential dropouts to stay in school until they're eighteen or twenty, won't solve anything; it could even make matters worse. In one sense, the dropouts show better judgment in dropping out than educators do in planning campaigns urging them to return. For the dropouts weren't learning anything when they were in school— nor, for the most part, were the schools terribly eager to keep them. In a group of dropouts studied by Professor S. M. Miller of Syracuse University, 90 percent of the boys were at least one grade behind the one they should have been in; nearly two-thirds were two or more grades behind. And a statewide study in Maryland indicated that nearly half the dropouts were reading at or below the sixth-grade level.

This academic failure, it should be emphasized, is not because the dropouts are unable to learn; at least two-thirds of them have I.Q.'s within the normal range. Since I.Q. tests substantially understate the native ability of youngsters coming from impoverished backgrounds, the proportion who should have been able to keep up is undoubtedly a good bit higher. And the dropouts *do* come predominantly from impoverished families. In the United States as a whole, 28 percent of the youngsters entering high school now drop out. (Another 5 percent leave *before* they enter high school.) But the high school dropout rate runs as low as 8 percent in a settled middle- and upper-income, white-collar suburb like Pasadena, California, and as high as 38 percent in an industrial city like Detroit. More to the point, perhaps, the dropout rate in Detroit's slum neighborhoods—or in New York's, Chicago's, Philadelphia's, or any other large city's—runs as high as 60 to 70 percent.

"College boys" and "corner boys"

Some slum children do succeed in school. But their academic success is not based solely on intelligence; it involves, as well, an ability (and desire) to leave the slum psychologically at an early age. In his *Street Corner Society,* a now classic analysis of Italian teenage society of the 1930s, the sociologist William F. Whyte raised the question of why some of the children of Italian immigrants became successful lawyers or businessmen, while others stayed mired in the slums—in Whyte's phrase, remained "corner boys." "The most obvious explanation," he wrote, "is that . . . a college education is tremendously important for social and economic advancement." But that was "only a part of the story. Most of the college men were set apart from their fellows as early as the ninth grade. When they were still children, they fitted into a pattern of activity leading toward social mobility. College education was simply a part of that pattern.

"Both the college boy and the corner boy want to get ahead," Whyte explained. "The difference between them is that the college boy either does not tie himself to a group of close friends or else is willing to sacrifice his friendship with those who do not advance as fast as he does. The corner boy is tied to his group by a network of reciprocal obligations from which he is either unwilling or unable to break away."

The corollary is that the youngster who doesn't attune himself at an early age to middle-class values finds school a more and more hostile place. Indeed, to understand the dropouts' difficulties, particularly their sullen anger and aimless way of life, one must realize that the schools' failure is not just a failure to teach. It is more terrible; for the schools *do* teach these children something: namely, that they are incapable of learning. Or so it seems to the children. They begin this lesson in the first grade, when they have trouble learning to read. The curriculum is based on the assumption that youngsters come to school already equipped with a wide range of verbal skills and concepts that are needed for learning to read—skills and concepts that middle-class children have imbibed with the air they breathe, but that most slum children have not yet acquired. This failure to learn to read becomes an increasing handicap as the youngsters go through school, for the amount of required reading increases at something like a geometric rate. It is not just their academic failure that oppresses, however. Edgar Friedenberg documents with devastating detail (in *Coming of Age in America*) the ways in which school organization itself seems calculated to show contempt for the students.

The result, as Robert Schrank of Mobilization for Youth has written, is that the life history of teenage slum dwellers has been "a continuum of failure." Lower-class dropouts, particularly Negroes and Puerto Ricans, "do not want to fail," Schrank argues, "and yet they know nothing else." This affects the youngsters' ability to perform on the job as well as in school. For the dropouts, as Schrank puts it, "have been conditioned to the idea that they are stupid." More important, they "have been conditioned to feel they are not capable of solving problems"; anything that smacks of problem-solving brings back what Schrank aptly terms "the reflex of failure." In sum, academic failure reinforces the slum young-ster's sense of being trapped by an alien and hostile world and persuades him that there is no way—certainly no legitimate way—for one of his background or his skin color to "make it" in the world at large.

4

The Drift to Early Retirement*

OF ALL THE DEVICES proposed for combating unemployment, few
are as plausible sounding as early retirement. Many labor unions
have recently won dramatic concessions at the bargaining table
designed to make the idea irresistible to older workers. The
nation's labor force, the unions point out, is expected to grow by
an unprecedented nine million persons between now and 1970,
with about half the increase occurring in the group aged fourteen
to twenty-four. The economy, they warn, may not grow fast
enough to absorb all these youthful job seekers. Suppose, however,
that some of the 13,300,000 workers who are now over fifty-five
retired sooner than they had planned.

More jobs for the young is not the only blessing claimed for
early retirement. Industry could gracefully rid itself of those older
employees who are said to be poor material for retraining in the
newest production techniques. The elderly workers themselves
would escape from grueling, monotonous work—a dividend of
leisure that our affluent society can well afford to declare. To
many, indeed, early retirement is only the logical extension of the
concept underlying mass pension plans, which presuppose that
most men no longer need to work until they drop dead. "God's
curse on Adam now runs out at sixty-five," says Ralph Helstein,
president of the United Packinghouse Workers. Why not, he asks,
bring down the retirement age still further?

So, bolstered by all these apparent advantages and beneficences,

* The author of this chapter is Edmund K. Faltermayer.

the idea has been growing apace. In 1964 the five major rubber companies, in negotiations with the United Rubber Workers, lowered the "normal" retirement age from sixty-five to sixty-two, i.e., a worker at this age can now get a pension without an actuarial reduction in his monthly payment; ordinarily, of course, a reduction would accompany any pension paid over a longer period of retirement. (As the chart on page 72 shows, the actuarial reductions can be quite drastic for early retirees.) The Oil, Chemical and Atomic Workers have won the same terms from Sinclair Oil Corp., and an official of the union terms the agreement a "giant step" toward making sixty-two the normal retirement age throughout the petroleum industry. Some unions have managed to eliminate the age requirement altogether. A member of the National Maritime Union with twenty years of shipboard duty, for example, can now leave with a $150-a-month pension at any age. A 1965 study by Bankers Trust Co. of New York City, one of the nation's largest managers of corporate pension funds, shows that 84 percent of a sampling of collectively bargained plans permit early retirement, with at least *some* pension, without the employer's consent (vs. 30 percent a decade ago).

Early retirement has caught on strongly in many industries where the work is especially arduous or monotonous. Since 1963 members of the Teamsters Union in certain parts of the country have been able to retire at fifty-seven without suffering any actuarial reduction in their pensions. In 1964, 27 percent of the retirees in these areas were under sixty. The United Mine Workers has lowered from sixty to fifty-five the age at which a man is eligible for a pension and boosted the monthly payment to $85. Thousands of miners have indicated they will quit early under the new plan.

"Early out" in Detroit

The most attractive early-retirement provisions of all are those won by the United Auto Workers. In the 1964 negotiations with the Big Three automobile companies, the U.A.W. demanded and got supplementary payments that give the early retiree a *bigger* pension than the man who retires at sixty-five. After September 1965 a sixty-year-old automobile worker with thirty years of service could retire on as much as $400 a month. (Under the old

contract he could have drawn only $54.26 a month.) It is signifi-
cant that the special supplements are available only during the
years before sixty-five, even for those who retire early. At sixty-
five, when the retiree can supplement his private pension by
drawing social security without an actuarial reduction, the pension
will drop back to the "normal" amount, which is $110.54 in the
case of the worker with thirty years' service. By offering a man
more now and less later, the union hopes to tide him over the years
when he might otherwise have earned $600 a month. The plan,
says U.A.W. President Walter Reuther, will make it possible for a
man and his wife "to enjoy a living standard that begins to
approach the living standard they had while he was working."

Since the avowed purpose of this early-retirement plan is to
open up jobs, it is important that those who opt for it do not come
back into the labor market. Under another unique new provision
the early retiree will lose his pension supplements if he earns more
than $1,200 a year from any job, automotive or otherwise. Union
men are optimistic that auto workers, who have shown a tendency
to retire early in recent years anyway, will take full advantage of
the new pensions. "In five more years," says Charles Odell,
director of the U.A.W.'s older and retired workers' department,
"there will be very few workers over sixty in the Big Three
companies."

Other unions have been pressing the early-retirement issue in
recent negotiations. On the West Coast, where employment in the
aerospace industry has hit a plateau, officials of both the Machinists Union and the Auto Workers won improved early-retirement
provisions in their negotiations with North American Aviation and
Lockheed late in 1965. "There is no single cure for the great
malady of unemployment," says Robert Simpson, who negotiated
for the Machinists with Lockheed, "but earlier retirement is one of
the very important things to be done."

Early retirement is sometimes being used at management's
initiative to get rid of a worker in a "red circle" job—i.e., one that
is to be eliminated by attrition. In this situation, a fattened-up
pension may cost the company less than keeping a superfluous
man on the payroll until he retires on his own or dies. Similarly, it
can also be used as a substitute for layoffs. The petroleum
companies, forced by competitive pressures to trim their payrolls

in the late 1950s, have used the device extensively. Standard Oil Co. (New Jersey), for example, credits a specially sweetened early-retirement program for one-third of the 12,000-man cutback it achieved in its refineries and offices between 1957 and 1962. In a typical case, a man of sixty with thirty years of service, who would have been eligible for an actuarially reduced pension of $182 a month, was offered a special $77 supplement to bring it up to $259. This was still not as much as the unsupplemented $332 pension the same man could have drawn if he had stayed on the job five years longer, but for many workers it was sufficient inducement to leave early. Because many of them did, fewer younger workers had to be laid off.

In addition to expanding employment opportunities for the young, its advocates say, early retirement opens up new vistas of leisure. "Who wants to see a man past sixty going into the depths of a copper mine to work a shift?" asks an official of the Mine, Mill and Smelter Workers in Denver. "Most of our men are pretty well shot by the time they reach sixty, let alone sixty-five." An official of the Teamsters Union calls retirement at fifty-seven "almost a physical necessity" for truck drivers. Many sociologists hail the trend toward more years of leisure, even for those whose work is not so onerous. "Leisure is an achievement of technology and of our way of life," says Woodrow W. Hunter of the University of Michigan, who has studied retirement patterns among blue-collar workers. "I have a strong feeling," says Clark Tibbitts, deputy director of the Office of Aging in the U.S. Department of Health, Education and Welfare, "that when we provide adequate income for retirement and sufficient cultural outlets, we're going to have a great deal more retirement prior to age sixty-five, and even prior to age sixty."

Some major barriers

But this is not likely to happen soon. In the years immediately ahead, it is extremely doubtful that early retirement can be expanded rapidly enough to open up millions of jobs for younger workers.

For one thing, little help can be expected from women, who account for about a third of the 13,300,000 older workers; the proportion of women aged fifty-five to sixty-four in the labor force—i.e., working or looking for work—has risen sharply, from 24.3 percent in 1948 to 40.2 percent in 1964. The only real hope lies with the 8,900,000 men in the labor force over fifty-five. These men, all but 4 percent of them employed in recent months, cannot be forced out of their jobs. Few advocates of early retirement are proposing that the mandatory retirement age, generally sixty-five, be lowered. The only way to remove these men from the labor force is to entice them to retire.

But the obstacles to this are formidable. First, there is the psychological barrier: many men, particularly those now in their fifties and sixties, would not know what to do with themselves if they left their jobs. Second, there is an economic obstacle. Most workers cannot even consider retiring without a pension to supplement their social security. But private pension coverage in the United States is still quite limited despite its phenomenal growth in recent years. Fewer than half the workers in private industry are covered, and the average benefit currently being paid is only about $95 a month. Even when workers are covered, the actuarial facts of life make it exceedingly costly for companies to offer adequate pensions to men who retire early. In most instances, says Martin E. Segal, president of a firm of pension-plan consultants and actuaries, "you must choose between reducing pension benefits to meaningless amounts, and increasing the cost of providing them by 150 to 300 percent."

Unquestionably, there has been some increase in the number of men who are retiring early. Those who profess to see a strong trend cite the increase in the number of men applying for their social security before sixty-five. In 1961, the privilege of applying as early as sixty-two, already available to women, was extended to men. In 1964, 49 percent of the retired men added to the Social Security Administration's rolls were under sixty-five. But some of those "early retirees" appear to be the unemployed under another name. A study published recently in the *Social Security Bulletin* said that "most of these men [were] in economically distressed circumstances." Many were in poor health and some were out of work. Only 11 percent of them said they retired early because they "preferred leisure." The decision to apply early for social security must have been a reluctant one for many of them, because those who begin drawing it before sixty-five suffer an actuarial reduction up to 20 percent in their monthly payments.

Voluntarily or not, the number of older men who have been retiring from the labor force does not suggest a stampede. This is made clear by government figures on labor-force "participation rates." For males between sixty and sixty-four—the group presumably most tempted to retire early—the rate declined only slightly between 1960 and 1964, from 81.2 percent to 79.1 percent. The fact is that most men in this age group who leave their jobs turn right around and get others if they can. A lot of today's early "retirees," in other words, are older men who are leaving arduous blue-collar jobs and supplementing their pension income with less demanding work as night watchmen, service-station attendants, and the like.

In sum, the news about early retirement is not that many workers are actually choosing it, but that more companies are *offering* it. And offering early retirement is not the same as encouraging it. Encouragement may take several forms: a lowering of the "normal" retirement age, pension supplements for early retirees, or both. But relatively few companies have lowered the normal retirement age. And a study of 1,099 pension plans by the National Industrial Conference Board revealed that in 1962 only about one-fourth offered supplements. The figure is undoubtedly higher now. Still, as the statistics on labor-force "participation rates" show, the various inducements are pulling few men below sixty-five out of the labor force.

The "leisure boom"

But may we not be on the verge of a considerable rush to early retirement during the critical years between now and 1970? The argument that we are is based not only on the fact that retirement incomes are improving but on the impression that more and more Americans are attracted to leisure as a way of life.

One indication is the reduction in the average work week in the United States and, more noteworthy of late, the shortening of the "work year" by means of additional paid holidays and longer vacations. The "work life" of men is also coming down as life expectancy goes up. During the decade of the 1950s the remaining life expectancy of a man who had attained age sixty increased a tenth of a year, to 15.8 years. But his remaining work-life expectancy, as computed in a Labor Department study, declined by 1.3 years, to 8.5 years. Accordingly, the number of years of retirement a man of sixty can anticipate has increased from 5.9 to 7.3.

But a close examination of the facts shows that leisure is not busting out all over in the United States—at least not yet. The government statistics generally cited, which show a decline in the average work week for nonagricultural employees from 39.6 hours in 1948 to 38 in 1960, reflect to some extent the growth in part-time work, most of it done by women. As Professor Sebastian de Grazia of Rutgers University points out in his book, *Of Time, Work, and Leisure,* the average nonagricultural employee with a full-time job—one involving at least thirty-five hours of work—actually put in 45.2 hours in 1960, only slightly less than the 45.6 hours he worked in 1948. (These figures are for May of the respective years.) A Labor Department study shows that the total leisure gained by the shortening of the work week and work year between 1940 and 1960 was equivalent to nearly twenty work days, which sounds fairly impressive. What is more impressive, however, is the amount of added leisure *not* being taken. Workers' productivity grew enormously in the United States during those two decades, but those four weeks represented only 11 percent of the total increase in gross national product theoretically made possible by this rise in efficiency.

They go grudgingly

Nor does the shortening of the average male work life indicate a sudden upwelling of interest in shuffleboard. Much of the shortening is involuntary and reflects industry's growing practice of making retirement mandatory at a certain age, usually sixty-five. Also reflected is the sharp increase in the proportion of older workers who are eligible for social security benefits when they retire, now about 80 percent of the total. Those who receive them—and nearly all of the eligibles do—are subject to a "retirement test" that, in effect, discourages most of them from earning more than

$1,200 a year. (As earnings rise above that figure, social security payments are reduced, and, above a certain level, eliminated completely.) The result, not surprisingly, has been a sharp decline in the proportion of men over sixty-five in the labor force, from 33.1 percent in 1960 to 28 percent in 1964.

However, the increased withdrawal of men over sixty-five from the labor force has been offset by the growing tendency of married women to work during their middle years. The result is that even though men are retiring sooner than they once did, the percentage of jobholders in the adult population has been staying fairly constant. The figure, in fact, has varied only slightly since 1890. "In almost three-quarters of a century of dramatic change in the United States," remarks Seymour L. Wolfbein, economic adviser to Secretary of Labor W. Willard Wirtz, in a recent book, "the economically active proportion of the [adult] population has remained about the same, somewhat over 50 percent." To those who believe Americans should cultivate leisure more, as Professor de Grazia does, we still seem to be a nation of moneygrubbers.

From the foregoing it is also clear that the men over sixty-five who are now in the labor force do not represent a major potential source of jobs for the younger generation. They number only 2,100,000 and many of them are farmers and professionals who are not subject to fixed retirement ages. If employment opportunities are to be opened up, we must concentrate on the age group between fifty-five and sixty-four, where an overwhelming 85.6 percent of the men, or 6,700,000 workers, are in the labor force. But here, even more than in the older group, the desire for leisure is fairly weak, and the attachment to one's job is often fairly strong.

This attachment to work has often been attributed to a "Protestant ethic." Dr. Harold L. Sheppard, of the W. E. Upjohn Institute for Employment Research, believes there has been "a lot of romanticizing of the work ethic," and doubts that it applies to blue-collar workers. Nevertheless, he adds, "people do feel uncomfortable when they're not working. It's partly guilt feelings, but also partly force of habit." Work forms an important part of many employees' social lives, even in certain production jobs. "The clothing industry is not a taxing one and it's gregarious," says a spokesman for the Amalgamated Clothing Workers, a union that is not pushing early retirement. "There is no real urgency on the part of our people to retire."

How might retirement be made attractive—or even palatable—to more older men? One answer is suggested by the results of an exhaustive study carried out during the 1950s by a team of Cornell University sociologists. They found "high morale" in 63 percent of those retirees enjoying good health and a high retirement income, but only in 33 percent of those with good health and a low retirement income. For many, then, the proposition turns on income.

But there's the rub. Even if all those 6,700,000 men in the labor force who are between fifty-five and sixty-four wanted leisure—and clearly not all of them do—only a minority could retire now on an income they would consider adequate. For many, retirement would mean a descent into poverty. The main source of income for most retirees is social security. This is not available until sixty-two, and the maximum benefit payable then for a man with a wife who has never worked is only $149.30 a month (vs. the $190.50 available to the man who retires at sixty-five). Since social security payments are based on past earnings, most early retirees get less than the maximum. Many supplement the payments by working, but they rarely earn more than the $1,200 a year permitted under the "retirement test." The study of early retirees in the *Social Security Bulletin* shows that the married couples had a median income from all sources of only $2,470 in 1962. This is below the $3,000 minimum that the Labor Department considers necessary to maintain a "modest but adequate" standard of living for an elderly couple. The average United States factory worker earns $5,355 in a year (before taxes).

Improvements are on the way, of course. Medicare will presumably ease retirees' worries about hospital bills. The 7 percent increase in social security benefits, which in 1965 was provided along with medicare, will also help a bit. But these gains will offset only a small part of the drop in income faced by the man who retires early.

The "elite" pensioners

What is really needed to grease the way to early retirement, then, is a good private pension. But Merton C. Bernstein of Yale

University, author of a book on pensions, says "there is not much grease available." Private pensions have grown enormously in recent years, with the number of workers covered—i.e., employed by companies that have plans—shooting up from 9,800,000 in 1950 to an estimated 25 million today. But this growth now appears to be slowing down. And coverage figures are deceptive anyway, because workers who are covered often wind up with very small pensions, or no pensions at all, if they have changed jobs often. Only about 2,400,000 persons actually received private pension payments in 1964—a sixth as many as received social security benefits. People with private pensions, says a study by the Social Security Administration, "constitute the economic elite" among the nation's retired.

Even for this elite, early retirement can impose severe penalties. The actuarial reduction or "discount" in a typical pension is heavy; and any effort to make it up would be costly. To make a pension that is now paid at sixty-five available five years earlier (making sixty the base year from which actuarial discounts are computed), a company would typically have to pay about 60 percent more into its fund. Lowering the age to fifty-five would raise costs approximately 135 percent.

Actuarial arithmetic is not the only thing going against most early retirees. In many companies, the majority of older workers have not worked long enough to qualify for a full pension. In the hypothetical plan shown in the chart on the next page, a man must put in twenty-five years to get $100 a month at sixty-five. A man of fifty-five with only fifteen years of service would get only three-fifths of his earned pension, already reduced actuarially to $46.30, or a piddling $27.78 a month—and would still have seven years to go before he could apply for social security!

Luring out the auto workers

The high cost of early retirement means that unions pushing for it must forgo other things—especially wage increases. In order to make a $150-a-month pension available after twenty years of service, regardless of age, the National Maritime Union had to pass up two annual wage increases totaling 5 percent that had already been agreed upon with management. And the United Auto

Chart 8. How Quitting Early Can Shrink a Worker's Pension

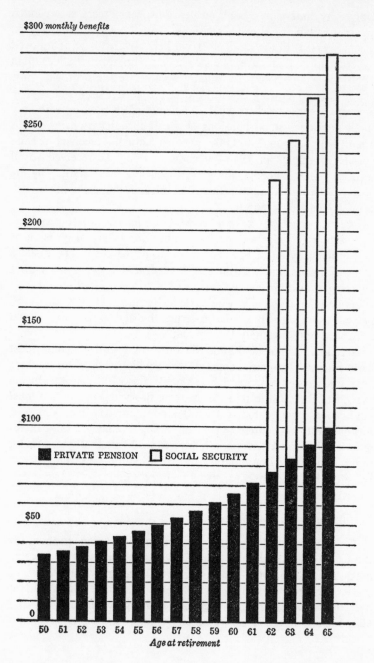

$300 *monthly benefits*

$250

$200

$150

$100

■ PRIVATE PENSION □ SOCIAL SECURITY

$50

0

50 51 52 53 54 55 56 57 58 59 60 61 62 63 64 65

Age at retirement

Workers, to get their spectacular early-retirement provisions, had to forgo the customary 2.5 percent "improvement factor" (i.e., wage increase) during the contract's first year.

With this kind of bait the U.A.W., not surprisingly, has been able to lure men out of the labor force. During the first three months after the pension supplements became available in September, 1965, some 10,000 workers at the four automobile companies elected to retire before sixty-five. While this is a significant number, it may reflect the desire to get away from assembly-line work, which is more grueling than most industrial jobs. It remains to be seen whether more automobile workers will take advantage of the new plan. The U.A.W. estimated in 1965 that a total of 30,000 men, or about 5 percent of all hourly rated employees, were eligible for early retirement with supplemented pensions. Not all of them, however, were eligible for the $400-a-month maximum, which is paid only to a man between sixty and sixty-four who has a base wage of at least $3.30 an hour and has put in thirty years of service.

Even when he is covered by a private pension plan, the early retiree has several things going against him. First, he cannot begin drawing social security until age sixty-two. Second, most companies make an actuarial reduction in his pension because they must pay it out to him over a longer period. The earlier the man retires, the bigger the bite— usually 6 to 7 percent for each year prior to the man's normal retirement age.

Chart 8 shows how the squeeze works in a hypothetical but typical company, one that pays a $100-a-month pension to an average worker retiring at sixty-five. For simplicity, we assume that the workers have wives the same age who have never worked and no other dependents. We assume, further, that at sixty-five they are eligible for the maximum amount of social security (currently $190.50), i.e., the total retirement income is $290.50. Men who retire at sixty-two would get a company pension of $77.30, and their social security would be actuarially reduced too, giving a total of only $226.60. Men who retire at sixty are not yet eligible for social security, and their pension is only $66 a month. At fifty-five it's only $46.30, and at fifty a mere $34. But things can be even worse. We have assumed that these men have put in twenty-five years of service, the maximum for accumulating pension credits at this company. If a man of fifty had only fifteen years of service, his pension would be a minuscule $20.40 a month.

Many labor leaders favor an alternative to early retirement: bargaining to improve pensions for those who retire at sixty-five. This was what the United Steelworkers went after in their 1965 negotiations with the can companies. At first they called for pension supplements for early retirees, but then they made an interesting policy switch and settled for a sharp increase in the ordinary pension, to $5.50 a month per year of service (up from $3.25). This tops the "normal" $4.25 pension now available to auto workers. In their contract with the steel industry, the Steelworkers won retirement with full pension for workers with thirty years' service—an early-retirement incentive for those who qualify —but no pension supplements, as such, for early retirees.

Many companies also oppose making early retirement really attractive. New York City's Consolidated Edison Co. allows early retirement, but its heavily reduced pension payments deliberately discourage it. Caterpillar Tractor Co., which bargains with the United Auto Workers, refused to agree to the pension supplements Walter Reuther had won from the automobile industry. Instead, it will use an equivalent amount of money to boost normal retirement benefits to $6 a month per year of service—making its pensions among the highest in the United States for hourly rated employees. It did yield a bit by lowering the normal retirement age to sixty-two, but it resisted any features that would strongly induce employees to go before the mandatory age of sixty-six. The reason, says a spokesman, is that "we find people in their early sixties are damned good workers."

Between forty and ninety

Many who have wrestled with these problems are coming to believe that the best approach is neither early retirement as it is now being promoted nor compulsory retirement at sixty-five. Instead, it would be a highly flexible system that could take account of older workers' differing abilities and preferences for work or leisure. "People should be able to quit at forty or remain on the job until they are ninety," says Martin Segal. "There are men of sixty-five who are healthier than those of forty, and vice versa."

What many are suggesting, in effect, is that corporations adopt pension systems similar to the highly flexible one that covers federal employees. This permits a person to retire as early as fifty-five—but also allows him to stay on until seventy. The essential feature is that with each year that passes, even after sixty-five, the employee's pension becomes better. The retirement plan at Wm. Wrigley Jr. Co. is one of the few in private industry that offer this feature. Under plans of this type most men eventually reach a point at which retiring becomes irresistible.

In practice, however, most companies seem increasingly to prefer a fixed retirement age, on the ground that it prevents older workers from hanging on too long and also that it makes the pension plan easier to administer. But in a highly flexible system with good pensions the workers do not stay around forever; the average federal employee retires at sixty-one and the average worker at Wrigley at sixty-five. And Segal, among others, doubts that a flexible retirement system would really be harder to administer.

One side effect of the push for early retirement does seem eminently desirable: a worker who "retires" early enough can begin a second career if he wishes. This has been the pattern for years with members of the armed services, who generally can retire with good pensions in their forties. And one member of the National Maritime Union, who recently retired at thirty-eight, is now studying to become a policeman. Most such pensions are too small to live on, but they may still represent a useful supplement for a man who wants to shift to another job; he has, at least, more options in his life.

To many who have followed the current early-retirement push, it represents an ironic reversal of policy by some labor unions. During the years just after World War II, when there was a labor shortage, these unions put the emphasis on allowing older men to stay on the job *past* sixty-five. The switch, of course, has been prompted by the higher unemployment rates that prevailed until 1965. But the earlier policy is worth keeping in mind. "If unemployment fell," says Dr. Sheppard, "a lot of this current trend would go right out the window. Then you might need incentives to keep people *in* the labor force."

5

The Mixed-Up War on Poverty

"ONE OF THE most important and exciting things about the war on poverty," its commanding officer, Sargent Shriver, informed the Congress in the spring of 1965, "is that all America is joining in. Religious groups, professional groups, labor groups, civic and patriotic groups are all rallying to the call." It's not always clear, however, to which call "all America" is rallying. Indeed, the "war," which was then bathed in the warm glow of Lyndon Johnson's "great consensus," six months later was engulfed in bitter controversy; and there is every indication that the controversy will continue for some time.

The controversy has not involved the question of whether the federal government *should* be waging war on poverty; there is remarkably wide agreement that it should. There is agreement even among those who believe that the principal gains will continue to come, not from government action, but from the steady rise in productivity and output. Despite the widely publicized statements to the contrary, the number of people living in poverty has been declining, both absolutely and relative to total population. Between 1959 and 1964, for example, the number of people classified as poor under the Social Security Administration's poverty-income standard* declined by nearly five million (from

* The Social Security Administration's poverty-income standard takes family size and composition and place of residence into account; for an

38,900,000 to 34,100,000); the poor declined as a proportion of the population, too—from 22.1 percent in 1959 to 18.0 percent in 1964. In 1965 there was another sharp drop of approximately 1,500,000, bringing the proportion below 17 percent. The sharp rise in employment of blue-collar workers has helped this movement a lot.

Table 2. The Poor
(millions of people)

	Total population	Poor persons	Percent of total
1959	176.5	38.9	22.1
1960	179.5	40.1	22.3
1961	181.4	38.1	21.1
1962	184.4	37.0	20.1
1963	187.2	35.3	18.9
1964	189.7	34.1	18.0

SOURCE: Annual report of the Council of Economic Advisers, 1965, p. 111.

But the process is far too slow to satisfy the consciences of most Americans who live in relative comfort. A substantial number of Americans are still poor. Some of them—for example, the aged, the infirm, and husbandless mothers—benefit little from economic growth, since they are outside the labor market. Others are employed, but their skills are so meager that they cannot look forward to more than a succession of badly paid and frequently demeaning jobs. And through lack of education, discrimination, and their own conviction that the cards are stacked against them, the "children of poverty" are all too often condemned to repeat their parents' fate. Clearly, therefore, as a U.S. Chamber of Commerce Task Force on Economic Growth and Opportunity put it, "Poverty is significant enough to make its alleviation a prime social and national goal."

The question is how. Shriver and his lieutenants are very much aware of criticisms that have been leveled recently against the "welfare industry" in the United States, and of a widening convic-

---

urban family of four (two adults, two children), the standard works out to about $3,100 a year. The standards are adjusted to take account of changes in the purchasing power of the dollar over the period analyzed above.

tion that it really does little to help the poor; and they have tried to make it clear that *this* program is not just more of the same. It will try to change local governmental and voluntary welfare institutions in a number of ways, and it will add new services and approaches. "The major focus," says Sanford L. Kravitz, chief of research and program development for the community-action programs, "must be on placing leverage under a broad series of institutions for basic attention to the problems of the poor."

The leverage is in Section 202 (a) (3) of Title II of the Economic Opportunity Act of 1964, under which the war on poverty is being waged. In general, Title II is designed to "provide stimulation and incentive for urban and rural communities to mobilize their resources to combat poverty." The "stimulation and incentive" take the form of money: the Office of Economic Opportunity pays up to 90 percent of the cost of local community-action programs. But the programs must be "developed, conducted, and administered with the maximum feasible participation of residents of the areas and members of the groups" for whose benefit the act was passed. "One of the major problems of the poor," OEO's Community Action Workbook states, "is that they are not in a position to influence the policies, procedures, and objectives of the organizations responsible for their welfare." The "maximum feasible participation" clause gives OEO a mandate to correct that problem—to see to it that the poor do have a say in the planning and operation of welfare programs.

The meaning of involvement

Almost all the controversy over the program stems from that mandate. Some critics are complaining that all those high-flown statements about involving the poor are hypocrisy—that the poor are participating only in token fashion. Others are complaining that the poor are too deeply involved. The disagreement has been partly over the facts, but primarily over the meaning of "participation"—and over whether the mandate should have been included in the first place.

What does "maximum feasible participation" of the poor really mean? What, in any case, do Shriver and his staff *think* it means, and how do they intend to carry out their mandate? The latter questions are perhaps more relevant because the section itself is so vague that Shriver, like the Queen in *Alice in Wonderland,* can make the words mean pretty much what he wants.

What he wants seems to vary. His speeches and statements have not been entirely consistent, nor have the criteria OEO has invoked in approving or rejecting local programs. On some occasions Shriver has suggested that the poor must be deeply involved in every phase of the program—that they not only must have decision-making responsibility, but may even be looked to for a kind of moral leadership. In January 1965 he cautioned against "trying only to remake the poor in our own image," and added, "The problems of poverty will not be solved until we acknowledge that the poor have as much or more to give than they get—in insight, in culture, in spontaneity, and in basic humanity." Moreover, he says he feels "a personal commitment to ensure that the poor themselves actively participate in the planning, implementation, and administration of these programs." All too often, he notes, statutory clauses requiring "citizen participation" have been "turned into meaningless exhortations and formalities where the poor are asked or required to assent to programs that they neither comprehend nor desire." Hence involvement of the poor must mean "giving them effective power, a respected and heeded voice and genuine representation in all aspects of the program and at all stages in the significant decision-making processes."

There are two ways of doing this, says the OEO workbook. One is by appointing poor people to positions within the community-action agencies themselves—positions "that permit the poor to influence the objectives, policies, actions, and services of the organization." The other is "to assist the poor in developing autonomous and self-managed organizations which are competent to exert political influence on behalf of their own self-interest"—for example, by developing "associations based on common problems and grievances" or by "reinforcing existing organizations directly managed by the poor."

What really alarms the mayors

Many Americans, however, do not believe that the poor are competent to influence community-action agencies, let alone run their own organizations. Putting poor people in positions of influence in a community-action agency, Chicago's Mayor Richard J. Daley contemptuously told reporters, "would be like telling the fellow who cleans up to be the city editor of a newspaper." "You can't go to a street corner with a pad and pencil and tell the poor to write you a poverty program," Mrs. Anne Roberts, staff director of New York City's anti-poverty board, says, "They wouldn't know how."*

More to the point, however, a good many mayors believe that it is *improper* for the federal government to involve the poor in the ways indicated in the workbook. The mayors have concentrated their fire on OEO's recommendation (in some cities, its insistence) that each community-action program be administered by an agency on whose board representatives of the poor and of the large voluntary institutions may form a majority. Public funds, the mayors argue, should be spent only by officials accountable to the taxpayers. What really alarms the mayors, however, is the prospect that use of federal power to "invest the poor with self-managed and independent political influence" will undermine *their* power and influence, which is based in good measure on control of the local welfare apparatus. At the annual meeting of the U.S. Conference of Mayors in June 1965 Mayors John F. Shelley of San Francisco and Samuel W. Yorty of Los Angeles, both Democrats, introduced a resolution accusing OEO of "fostering class struggle." OEO's insistence that "the poor must dominate this thing," Shelley warned, would have the effect of "wrecking the program" by removing it from the control of city officials. "The elected city officials must retain control."

What the mayors fear, in effect, is another large redistribution of political power in the cities. Their own power has been associated with the growth of the welfare state since the 1930s, which has meant a vast funneling of federal, state, and local money through their offices. Now, the mayors perceive, the war on poverty may bring about another shift in which the poor would look to Washington—or to their own organizations. Either way, they would be less amenable to the influence of City Hall.

* In May 1966, four and a half months after John V. Lindsay took office as mayor, Mrs. Roberts submitted her resignation.

Five minutes to participate

At the same time, paradoxically, uncertainty over just what OEO means by "maximum feasible participation" has got some people concerned that politically sophisticated mayors are turning the community-action program to their own political advantage. In cities like Chicago, Cleveland, and Detroit, the mayor controls the local community-action agency. William H. Robinson, a former Republican member of the Illinois legislature, now on the staff of the Church Federation of Greater Chicago, charges that in Chicago "the poverty program already has become a tool for powerful aldermen to use to control the poor." New York Governor Nelson Rockefeller expressed a similar kind of concern on June 24, 1965, when he wrote Shriver attacking part of New York City's community-action program—that part that would establish six "Community Progress Centers" in slum areas, manned largely by nonprofessionals. In four of the neighborhoods, Rockefeller pointed out, residents had already established their own self-help groups, and the city's centers would destroy these. The result, Rockefeller charged, would be to weaken participation by the poor but to strengthen the city's Democratic machine. "A superimposed community center, controlled by City Hall," the Governor wrote, "has the potential of developing into another political clubhouse with the 'block worker' acting the role of ward captain."

Politics aside, a number of people who are deeply committed to the concept of citizen participation doubt that OEO really expects to implement the concepts expressed in its workbook. They point to the fact that Shriver and his lieutenants have sometimes spoken as though "maximum feasible participation" could mean simply employing some poor people. Sometimes, furthermore, OEO's interest in involvement of the poor looks like a grandstand gesture. In addressing the National Conference on Poverty in the Southwest in January 1965, for example, Shriver proudly noted the presence and "the genuine involvement" of the poor. (Some 171 of them—they were actually given green badges to distinguish them from other guests—had been invited to attend the conference, and a dozen or so had five minutes each to talk about their problems and grievances.) "We did not come here with a federal checkbook," he assured his listeners. "We did not come here with a federal blueprint! We did not come here to impose our views on you—to tell you what is best for the poor. We came, instead, to listen to the voices of the poor and the voices of those genuinely concerned about poverty." But as the conference's "Summary Report" acidly pointed out, "Unfortunately, Mr. Shriver was unable to stay long enough to hear the voices of the poor" in the session scheduled after his address; instead, he "boarded his plane almost immediately to return to Washington."

Some critics, therefore, are so cynical as to view the talk about "participation" as just so much rhetoric masking a bureaucratic power struggle; the only real issue is who gets to run the welfare industry. In Chicago, according to the Reverend Lynward Stevenson, president of The Woodlawn Organization, a Negro community group set up without *any* government help, "there is no war on poverty; there is only more of the ancient galling war against the poor." And Saul D. Alinsky, executive director of the Industrial Areas Foundation, under whose aegis T.W.O. was created, charges that the poverty program is "a huge political pork barrel" being used "to suffocate militant independent leadership and organizations that might threaten the establishment."

How far can the government go?

It is not surprising that leaders of The Woodlawn Organization have been skeptical of the poverty program, for the success of their own program has rested on the use of tactics that the federal government would have difficulty emulating. Alinsky, for example, believes firmly that the poor have to help themselves—that, indeed, they can be helped in no other way—but that they have to be organized to do so. In practice, this has meant getting them deeply involved in boycotts, picketing, rent strikes, and other forms of protest designed to dramatize their grievances and to persuade them that they can improve their circumstances through their own efforts. These tactics are necessary, in Alinsky's view, because the basic characteristic of the city slum—its "life style," so to speak—is apathy, a cynical, worldly-wise conviction that "you can't fight City Hall."

Alinsky's analysis suggests that there are limitations on government's role in the war on poverty. Can one branch of government, in effect, organize militant protest against another? The federal government is doing this in one OEO project in Syracuse, and leaders of "indigenous" organizations in other cities clearly regard the "maximum feasible participation" clause as a promise of federal support for their activities. But the Syracuse project is still young; how far OEO will go in supporting militant protest against established institutions remains to be seen. OEO officials admit to some uncertainty; only time and experience, they argue, can determine the limits of federal supports for social protest.*

But if the government imposes *any* limits on the tactics of the poor, can it really be said that the poor are making the decisions? Or that they have "effective power"? The basic dilemma of the government's attempt to involve the poor, in short, is that it is obliged, to some extent, to be manipulatory and paternalistic; and manipulation and paternalism are precisely what the poor don't need.

Welfare for the not-so-poor

How did this question of involving the poor come up?

The starting point was a growing disenchantment with "welfarism" among economists, social workers, and social planners— their recognition that the massive public and private social-work, social-welfare apparatus that has developed in the United States over the past forty years or so fails to relieve, and sometimes even aggravates, the problems of poverty. Government welfare expenditures have risen to perhaps $30 billion a year, but scarcely anyone believes today that these vast sums do much to reduce poverty.

The poverty planners have identified three general explanations for the failure of welfarism in this respect. One is the middle-class bias of many welfare programs and institutions. A second is the

---

* The limits, it is now clear, are very narrow. On November 30, 1965 —after only nine months of operation—OEO turned down the project's request for a fifteen month extension of direct funding. (The project had been conceived as taking a minimum of two years.) OEO instead funded the project for only ninety days and urged its directors to apply for longer-term funding to the local community action agency, which had repeatedly attacked the project.

fragmentation and lack of coordination of the multifarious government and private services that are offered the poor. Finally, there is the fact that the poor are rarely given any say in what services will be offered them, or how they will be operated.

It has often been noted that the welfare state does not primarily benefit the poor. The farm price-support program, for example, subsidizes people not because they are poor but because they are farmers. The rationale is that farmers as a group have low incomes; but the poorest of the farm families—those that grow crops for their own subsistence—get almost no help. Similarly, social security functions largely as a compulsory insurance system for the benefit of the middle class. Income is redistributed, to be sure—but from young to old, not from rich to poor. Some 15 percent of the aged, moreover, receive no benefits at all, and only 10 percent of those who do draw benefits get the maximum. Other welfare-state institutions also tend to ignore those who need help the most. The federal and state employment services, for example, have little contact with the very poor. The same is true of most manpower training programs. Urban renewal has tended to uproot the poor to provide housing for middle- or upper-income families.

Serving the middle class

Nongovernment welfare institutions display much the same bias—a fact documented in some detail in a study of Detroit's welfare agencies made by Greenleigh Associates, a consulting firm specializing in welfare problems. Fewer than 4 percent of a sample of poor families interviewed by the Greenleigh team, for example, had had any contact with a voluntary agency. There is, in fact, a paucity of agency facilities in slum neighborhoods, since historically most voluntary agencies have followed their clients as they moved away from slums to better neighborhoods. More important, as the Greenleigh report puts it, the Detroit agencies, with a few notable exceptions, "prefer to serve a clientele that is in proportion to the normal socio-economic distribution of the population in the community," i.e., a predominantly middle-class clientele.

One objective of the community-action program, therefore, is to get government and voluntary institutions to refocus their efforts.

The workbook advises community-action agencies that "services and assistance are to be limited to families and individuals living in poverty."

Another large problem with welfarism has been the fragmentation of services among different agencies and jurisdictions that operate independently of, and sometimes at cross-purposes with, one another: welfare departments, school systems, employment services, training programs, counseling agencies, etc. This fragmentation means that agencies are able to deal only with individual aspects of the poverty problem; they never see the problem whole.

The remedy is coordination and planning, in OEO's view. "Since the causes of poverty are complex," Shriver informed Congress, "the solutions must be comprehensive. An illiterate adult must learn to read and write before he can enter the skill-training program that will lead to employment. The mother on welfare cannot enter employment or manpower training unless there is a day-care or community-school program for her children. The sixteen-year-old youth might not be dropping out of school if he had learned to read earlier or if a work-study program were available. Poverty is a web of circumstances, not the simple result of a simple condition."

A second major objective of the community-action program, therefore, is to induce communities to view poverty as a series of interlocking problems and to develop comprehensive plans for their solution that involve the major public and private institutions—particularly the public school system, the welfare department, the state employment service, the health department, and large private agencies like the Y.M.C.A., family-service associations, and settlement houses. In principle, at least, the local community-action programs can be approved only if they provide for "the re-direction, extension, expansion, or improved utilization" of existing activities or the development of new ones.

To encourage communities to develop effective long-range programs, OEO offers grants both for "program development" and for operations. Communities that can't pull all the elements together in a single coordinated program at the outset are advised to use a "building block" approach, starting with just a few essential services and adding others later. OEO hopes eventually to bring under its own umbrella every important public and private program affecting the poor, not just those it funds or supervises directly. The heads of all federal agencies are required by the Economic Opportunity Act to give preference in the allocation of funds to projects that are associated with a community-action program. (OEO has identified close to 200 federal programs that *could* be coordinated in this way, and it has drawn up an inventory of all the state, local, and voluntary programs affecting the poor.)

The view from below

But it is the fact that the poor are not consulted about what services are offered to them or how they are run, more than anything else, that accounts for the failure of welfarism to relieve poverty. The poor, as Professor Warren Haggstrom of Syracuse University puts it, "are usually being caught up in someone else's social reality." Their own view of reality is scarcely ever embodied in welfare services, and the officials who run these services seldom take kindly to suggestions from their "clients." All too often, social workers convey a sense of superiority, a patronizing "white man's burden" attitude that offends the most thick-skinned slum-dweller. By conveying to the poor the message that they are dependent and inferior, social workers and the programs they direct frequently manage to create or reinforce the very sense of dependency they are supposed to eliminate. This message is communicated in many different ways: by the old, unscrubbed buildings in which programs are housed; by the interminable waiting on hard benches; the indifference or rudeness of the people who are supposed to be helping, the thoughtless rules and the unconscious slights and snubs that drive home to the poor the fact that they are receiving charity. Sometimes rudeness passes into near-brutality. For example, welfare departments in Arizona, Colorado, Washington, D.C., and in a number of other cities and states, regularly raid their clients' apartments in the middle of the night to see if a man is present, and they search the closets and even the attics for men's clothing. The presence of an able-bodied man makes a family ineligible for relief—a rule that contributes substantially to family breakdown. Indeed, relief applicants are frequently told that the only way they can receive help is for their unemployed or unemployable husbands to abandon them. In many cities, moreover, any money a child may earn is deducted from the family's relief payments—a practice hardly likely to stimulate youngsters to look for jobs.

It is in an effort to get their own "social reality" fed into welfare planning that the poor are to be involved in the poverty program. And it is this objective, more than anything else, that gives the war on poverty its distinctive cast and tone.

"Tree watching" and "woods watching"

How well is OEO succeeding in its objectives? In Shriver's judgment, superbly. "I would guess that no federal government program in peacetime has ever gone so far so fast, nor ever zeroed in so well," he modestly suggests. Shriver concedes some minor flaws—"no one ever ran a war without any casualties"—but thinks there has been too much "tree watching" by the press and not enough "woods watching," as he terms it. "It's like a shooting war. A foot soldier may be pinned down on Omaha Beach and thinks the war is going against him. He doesn't realize that General Patton may be fifty miles inland, but only Eisenhower knows what the total picture is. And the whole war on poverty must be seen just that way."

But which are the trees and which the woods; what are the criteria by which OEO's performance should be judged?

Without doubt, a great deal has been accomplished in a short period of time. For one thing, the program has helped break through a kind of complacency that had blinded most Americans to the fact that poverty remains the condition of life for many. Specifically, several existing anti-poverty programs have been expanded and redirected toward the poor, and a number of promising new programs have been established, some of them incorporating ideas that reformers had been proposing for years. Among them are the Neighborhood Youth Corps, offering part-time jobs to school dropouts and to youngsters for whom the job may mean the possibility of staying in school; the college work-study program, which does the same for college students from low-income families; the Job Corps, offering remedial education and vocational training to school dropouts in a residential program; a program to create "neighborhood law firms" in a number of cities so as to provide poor people with a kind of legal aid never before available; and the effort to employ slum residents in nonprofessional social-service jobs, which should help to break down much of the exaggerated professionalism, paternalism, and inbred guild atmosphere that makes so much social work futile.

Where the opportunities are

But the real test of OEO's success will be its ability to change existing institutions—in particular, the public schools, the state employment services, and the welfare departments. Unless these institutions change, and change radically, the over-all improvement in social services is bound to be slight. And so far, at least, the OEO reformers are not getting as much reform as is needed—or as is being claimed.

A good case in point is the "neighborhood service center"—the decentralized "little City Halls" or "supermarkets of social services," as they are sometimes called—that OEO urges most big cities to establish as the principal operating arms of their community-action programs. The idea is a good one: to put all the agencies offering service to the poor together in a single building and to put the building in the neighborhood where the people to be served actually live (instead of having it downtown). The execution is something else again. The new centers have been planned and put together so hastily that real improvements in service are hard to find.

What they have most conspicuously improved is the salary level of the people who work there; whatever it may do for the poor, the war on poverty is the best thing that's happened to social workers since the New Deal was established. For there is now a gigantic sellers' market for social workers, welfare administrators, and "consultants" on welfare problems. In the long run, of course, this may be a considerable gain; in the past social workers have been poorly paid, and higher salaries might attract abler people. The short run is something else again; the supply of trained personnel can't be increased overnight, and so community-action programs are being staffed in the main by offering higher salaries to lure people away from existing agencies.* One result has been to create a great deal of cynicism among the poor.

"Dejected with his lot"

In many cities, in fact, the neighborhood centers are little more than facades behind which agencies conduct welfare business as usual. Chicago's new, much-publicized "urban progress centers" are organized, furnished, and operated in ways that make it clear nothing is really changing. What it means to be poor and dependent upon one of these centers for help is suggested by summaries of two case histories. (The summaries are *Fortune*'s; however, the U.P.C. director involved had selected the cases as typical.)

Mrs. R. had paid a month's rent in advance for a new apartment. When she moved in she found that there was no toilet as promised, the windows were broken, and the apartment generally was not ready for occupancy. When she asked the rental agent when the apartment would be ready, he put her off with vague answers. Ultimately she asked that her rental advance be returned. She was told that the rental agent was not authorized to make refunds; only the landlord himself could do that—but the agent refused to give her the landlord's name. When asked by a *Fortune* reporter what had been done, the U.P.C. "supervisor of follow-up" said the woman had been referred to the Legal Aid Society, whose representative told her she'd have to wait three weeks while he wrote a letter trying to determine the landlord's name.

Mr. M., a thirty-two-year-old Negro with a wife and seven children, was brought into the center by a nonprofessional "community representative"; the family was living without electricity in a debris-filled apartment; the children had not had a regular meal

---

* Shriver has offered statistics showing that the administrators of local poverty programs earn less than the heads of other city agencies or of voluntary social-service agencies. But he has not offered any figures comparing poverty-program salaries with the salaries their recipients got on their previous jobs.

in some time. It seems that Mr. M. had been placed by the Cook
County Department of Public Aid in a widely publicized program
to train drivers for the Yellow Cab Co., but was dropped after a
week or two when it was belatedly discovered that he was blind in
one eye. In the process the family's welfare payments were cut off.
As the U.P.C. staff member wrote, with apparent surprise, "Mr.
M. seems dejected with his lot in life." She referred Mr. M. to the
state employment-service representative at the center, who in turn
made an appointment for him to see still another representative in
the service's downtown office four days later. Mr. M. did not keep
the latter appointment because he managed to find a job loading
and unloading heavy scraps of metal. Far from being pleased, the
"community rep" was irritated by Mr. M.'s industry. The file bears
this notation: "It thus appears that Mr. M. did have carfare to
make his appointment, but was unwilling to motivate himself to
meet this commitment to obtain full-time employment." No attempt was made to schedule another appointment.

Shoring up the system

OEO officials admit candidly that so far the program has barely
made a dent in the welfare world. Change takes time, they argue—
particularly change in well-established institutions run by well-
entrenched bureaucracies—more time than the reformers have had
so far. The first community-action programs, OEO officials suggest, were bound to have a conventional design; the agency was
under too much pressure from Congress to get programs established and operating in a hurry, and so it could not take the time to
force communities to come up with creative and original pro-
posals. But none of this, they argue, precludes substantial change
later on. Community-action grants are made for only six to twelve
months; the power to refuse to renew the grants provides a weapon
the OEO reformers can use to bludgeon reluctant welfare departments, school boards, employment services, etc., into overhauling
their programs and procedures. What is crucial is "not the original
program design but the process."

It might be argued, however, that the "process" is not independent of the program; a badly designed program may impede or

even prevent the kind of institutional change OEO wants. The educational programs OEO is sponsoring, for example, do not provide for the kind of drastic overhaul that is plainly needed if the public schools are to educate children from low-income homes. They are designed, rather, to compensate for the schools' failures after they have occurred. The result, as one of our most eminent curriculum reformers puts it, is that OEO "is shoring up the same old stupid system, instead of changing it."

Moreover, Project Head Start, the one program that might lead to substantial reform, is being administered in a manner calculated to produce a maximum of publicity but a minimum of institutional change. The program underwrites the cost of eight-week preschool programs for over 500,000 youngsters due to enter school in the fall.* Preschool education is badly needed. There is a large and growing body of evidence that youngsters from low-income families perform badly in school because they enter lacking a good many specific skills and concepts (the ability to hold a pencil; the ability to recognize subtle differences in sound, e.g., between a "b" and a "p"; the concept of bigger and smaller) that they need before they can begin learning to read and write. What is needed, however, is *not* an extension of the conventional nursery school or day-care center, which offers little more than milk, cookies, games, and affection, but a curriculum that will teach them these skills and concepts. Unfortunately, Project Head Start will not be able to supply any such needs, for several reasons:

OEO tried to do too much too soon, in establishing an eight-week summer program in 1965 with only a few weeks or months of preparation. Because of the rush, teachers hired for the program were given an average of only six days of hurried training on how to "prepare the whole child for life."

The haste also blurred the program's objectives; providing medical care became the main point of the program. Providing such care for children who have never had it is surely a worthy objective; turning classrooms into clinics is something else again. The exaggerated claims and hucksterism with which the pro-

* Since this was written, Project Head Start has been expanded to include a year-round program for a much smaller number of children.

gram was surrounded have raised expectations that cannot be fulfilled. Shriver promised, in effect, that the 1965 summer's eight-week program would enable a half-million slum children to enter school in September equipped to compete on equal terms with youngsters from middle-class homes. But when children from low-income families enter school, their performance runs at least six months behind that of children from middle-income homes; eight weeks of medical care and instruction by inadequately trained teachers cannot close the gap. The danger is that school boards, superintendents, and taxpayers may conclude that preschool education is a waste—or that slum children are incapable of learning.

A heavy price

In other respects, too, the processes OEO has set in motion are not working in the direction of the changes OEO wants. Its insistence that community-action agencies be broadly based, for example, may actually reduce the likelihood of real innovation. The policy is understandable enough; the greater the number of institutions involved in a community-action program, the greater its claim to legitimacy and local support—an important consideration, given the suspicion with which Americans view federal intervention. But this kind of legitimacy, as Professor Martin Rein of Bryn Mawr has pointed out, is usually bought at a heavy price—forgoing any radical change. Once a broad coalition is formed, the overriding need is to keep the coalition together, and that in turn means a search for issues on which competing institutions and interests can agree.

The pressures to approve or continue mediocre projects do not all come from the outside, however; some of the strongest come from OEO's own bureacratic problems. One pressure has been the agency's determination to spend all the funds appropriated for the fiscal year. The pressure is understandable; after all, Shriver's reports of "prudent, practical, focused, and patriotic" expenditures had persuaded the Administration to double his budget for the current fiscal year. In May and June of 1965, therefore, as the fiscal year was drawing to a close, OEO officials were frantically trying to get the money out without dithering unduly about program design. All told, nearly 60 percent of the year's community-action grants were made in June, the last month of the 1965 fiscal year.

And the same pressures that have led OEO to approve unsatisfactory programs during its first year are likely to prevent it from cutting off the flow of funds later on. The furious storm generated in New York City in June, 1965 when Governor Rockefeller threatened to veto part of the city's community-action program— Rockefeller was accused, in effect, of taking bread out of the mouths of poor people— gives some indication of what OEO itself would be up against if it cut off funds and thereby killed existing programs.

There is an irony in the importance that is regularly attached to OEO's grants. It lies in the fact that the funds the agency provides are not really large enough to persuade the institutions most in need of change to reform themselves. OEO pays 90 percent of the cost of the individual programs it approves—but these programs represent a very small part of the budget of any city's public school system or welfare department. New York City, for example, is receiving about $50 million for its poverty program; its welfare budget alone exceeds $800 million, and its public school budget is about $1 billion. Professor Rein suggests that it is likely to be the reformers who are influenced by the welfare institutions, not the other way around.

The difficulty of changing programs after they are started is greatest when the change involves participation by the poor. What tends to happen is that the poor are excluded from the initial planning process in an effort to rush the plan through—to get a jump on other cities competing for the federal funds. "If we had waited to get the poor on the board," the Reverend Hubert Locke, executive director of Detroit's Citizens Committee for Equal Opportunity, asks rhetorically, "would Detroit have gotten as much money as it did?" "The important thing is the program, not the representation," one of the three Negro members of Cleveland's anti-poverty board told local community leaders who were dissatisfied with the number of poor people involved. "We have to get the program moving; we can't waste time on hassles about representation."

Once a program is moving, however, its directors are still not likely to welcome critics demanding more participation. On the contrary, the directors naturally take pride in the program they've drawn up and got approved; they identify with it and feel obliged to defend it. The longer a program is operating, moreover, the greater the pressure to mute criticism. Any leader of an indigenous slum organization who criticizes the program is likely to find his strength impaired as his followers—now dependent on some new job or service they fear to lose—urge silence, or simply leave the organization altogether. The result is that tentative participation ends up as acquiescence. Thus a great deal of effort is expended to get as many people as possible "participating."

Searching for the problem

There is still another large reason for doubting that the community-action program will change the welfare system as extensively or as deeply as the OEO reformers want: the fact that there is a good deal of uncertainty about the ultimate goal of the program. As Professor Burton A. Weisbrod of the University of Wisconsin has pointed out, it is called the war on poverty, but the agency conducting the war is called the Office of Economic Opportunity. "More than semantics is involved," Weisbrod argues. "As some people see it, *the* problem is inequality of opportunity—in education, in training, in employment; but to others the problem is the existence of living standards which are deemed abhorrent *whatever* the cause." Is the problem the unequal opportunities with which people enter the competition for income in the United States; or is the problem the *outcome* of that competition, regardless of cause? These concerns are not mutually exclusive, of course, but they involve quite different judgments about the proportion of federal money to be devoted to alleviating poverty and *preventing* poverty. And this judgment, in turn, involves another, about how funds should be spent. Should they be given directly to the poor, to raise their incomes above the poverty line? Or should the funds be invested in education and training for them or their children?

By and large, OEO's main emphasis has been on the latter. The agency's programs, Shriver has said, are "not aimed at amelioration of the hardships suffered by those in poverty, though they will bring such amelioration to many." But here again Shriver has been not quite consistent: when OEO is criticized for moving too rapidly, his reply, in effect, has been that the agency has to do *something* to help all those people who are suffering.

Perhaps the program's goals are fuzzy because Shriver and his lieutenants have never really decided what the causes of poverty really are or how they can be remedied. Former Assistant Secretary of Labor Daniel P. Moynihan has pointed out that "the war on poverty began on the basis of the undisputed persistence of poverty in the United States, but without any agreed-upon explanation for this fact." The closest one can come to any underlying rationale for the program lies in the testimony Walter Heller, then chairman of the Council of Economic Advisers, gave to a congressional subcommittee conducting hearings on the original antipoverty bill in 1964. The new tax cut, Heller argued, would speed up the rate of economic growth and thus open exists from poverty at a faster pace. "But open exits," he continued, "mean little to those who cannot move—to the millions who are caught in the web of poverty through illiteracy, lack of skills, racial discrimination, broken homes, and ill health—conditions which are hardly touched by prosperity and growth." In other words, the problem is *not* that the economy is failing to create enough jobs: "A surprisingly large percentage of poor persons already have some kind of job," Heller explained; for them, the cause of poverty "is not lack of jobs but lack of higher skills and productivity needed to yield a decent income. . . . They must be equipped with the knowledge, skills, and health to find and hold better jobs."

But to what extent will better jobs actually be available if the poor are equipped with "knowledge, skills, and health"? OEO seems to assume to a considerable extent, but that assumption rests on one of two others: that there is now a large unfilled demand for people with skills and education; or that increasing the supply of such people will itself increase the demand for them. As was argued in Chapter 2, there is little foundation for the first assumption. To be sure, there is *some* unfilled demand for labor, but much of it is for precisely the kinds of jobs poor people already hold: domestic servants, dishwashers, hospital attendants, and similar low-paying jobs.

What about the other assumption—that increasing the supply of people with education or job skills will increase the demand for skilled labor? Over the long run, supply does seem to create its own demand; education tends to increase productivity, thereby contributing to a faster rate of economic growth. Whether increasing the number of trained workers will increase demand for them in the short run, however (which is when those already out of school need help), is quite another matter. At best, the question is unresolved.

The tragic flaw

It is also undiscussed—at least in public. In private some OEO staffers admit to doubt; they lean on a vague expectation that if the people who are trained do *not* find jobs, they will at least generate enough political pressure to force the government to create jobs for them. One result of this uncertainty is that a good many programs —e.g., the Neighborhood Youth Corps—seem designed less to teach specific job skills or to create jobs than to "improve employability" or "increase motivation." But "motivation" is not a skill that can be taught, and efforts to teach it result in programs that are maddeningly vague and unhelpful.

In the end, the community-action program will succeed or fail, not on its record in delivering more or better social services, but on its record in involving the poor—in persuading them that they can control their own environments. Thus far, it must be said, the tragic flaw of paternalism remains. "I warn you against doing good to people," Jane Addams said thirty-five years ago. "One does good, if at all, *with* people, not *to* them." The warning still holds.

6

Is Technology Taking Over?

*It is an illusion—unfortunately very widespread—to think
that because we have broken through the prohibitions, taboos,
and rites that bound primitive man, we have become free.
We are conditioned by something new: technological civilization.*

—JACQUES ELLUL

*All values apart, we must learn today that our electric tech-
nology has consequences for our most ordinary perceptions
and habits of action which are quickly recreating in us the
mental processes of the most primitive men.*

—MARSHALL MCLUHAN

"MAN RUSHES FIRST to be saved *by* technology," the novelist
Gerald Sykes has written, "and then to be saved *from* it." Of late,
the latter rushing has been more noticeable; indeed, Man as Victim
of his Technology is emerging as one of the most insistent and
characteristic themes of our time. Fear of technology lay at the
root of the gloomy talk about automation and unemployment that
filled the mass media in the early 1960s. It was manifest in the
1965 student revolts at Berkeley and elsewhere: "I am a human
being; do not fold, bend, or mutilate," the students had written on
the signs they carried. The fear erupted in the wake of the massive
power failure that blacked out New York City and most of the
Northeast in November 1965. "The British author E. M. Forster
once drew a frightening picture of a civilization that surrendered to
automation, then collapsed from the weight of its own complex-

ity," the New York *Times* science editor, Walter Sullivan, recalled, adding, "The consequences of [the] electric blackout have given new meaning to this vision."

The theme is hardly new; men have always felt an irresistible urge to try to master nature and have always harbored a deep-seated fear that the attempt would anger the gods and bring about their own downfall. This ambivalence is one of the most persistent themes of mythology and legend. The price of eating of the Tree of Knowledge—of daring "to be as God"—was expulsion from Eden. For daring to give man the gift of fire, Prometheus was condemned to savage torture. And every age has had its own variation on the theme of the sorcerer's apprentice: the young apprentice, too lazy to fill his master's water barrel by his own labor, invokes some fragments of an incantation he has overheard and puts the broom to work fetching water. The broom does so with dispatch; but soon the barrel begins to overflow, and the lad, ignorant of the incantation needed to stop the broom, is powerless to intervene.

In the traditional version, the sorcerer returns in time to stop the broom and save the boy from drowning. In the contemporary myth, however, disaster seems to be irreversible; it is inherent in the technologies man creates. "During the past two centuries," writes the English social scientist, Sir Geoffrey Vickers, "men gained knowledge and power," which they used "to make a world increasingly unpredictable and uncontrollable." The belief that increased power to alter the environment permits increased control over it "is a manifest delusion," Sir Geoffrey argues, adding, "The rate of change increases at an accelerating speed, without a corresponding acceleration in the rate at which further responses can be made; and this brings ever nearer the threshold beyond which control is lost."

In the opinion of some, control has already been lost. The French sociologist Jacques Ellul has announced in *The Technological Society* that "a technical take-over" has occurred, and that it is irreversible. Ellul's American translator and advocate, John Wilkinson of the Center for the Study of Democratic Institutions, writes of an "autonomous technology" that is said to be "taking over the traditional values of every society without exception, subverting and suppressing these values to produce at last a monolithic world culture in which all nontechnological difference and variety is mere appearance." According to Ellul and Wilkinson, men can no longer turn technology to their own ends; rather, it "has become an end-in-itself, to which men must adapt themselves"—even though the process subverts so many human values. Technology has placed itself "beyond good and evil"; indeed, it has such "power and autonomy . . . that it, in its turn, has become the judge of what is moral, the creator of a new morality." The result is bound to be the dehumanization of man himself. When "the edifice of the technical society" is completed, Ellul grimly concludes, "the strains of human passion will be lost amid the chromium gleam."

This degree of pessimism is extreme, of course. But the unquestioning optimism that marked so much nineteenth-century talk about technology has virtually disappeared. An optimist nowadays is someone who thinks we have a pretty good chance to solve the problems posed by technology; he is nevertheless apt to betray a certain brooding uneasiness about the future. "Can We Survive Technology?" the late John von Neumann asked in the title of an essay he wrote in 1955 as part of *Fortune*'s twenty-fifth anniversary celebration. His answer was yes, but there was no doubt that he regarded the question as a real one.

The prospect of "dehumanization" is not the only concern about technology being expressed these days. Another arises out of the possibility of nuclear destruction. A third concern has to do with the future of democracy, the argument being that ordinary citizens and government officials are losing the capacity to understand national policy decisions. The English scientist-turned-novelist, C. P. Snow, is perhaps the best known of those who hold that critical governmental decisions now involve such complex technical questions that only scientists are capable of making them. Finally, there is the specter of mass idleness—i.e., the fear that automation of production and distribution will eliminate the need for human labor. Some writers see this primarily as an economic problem. Others view it as primarily social or psychological and have argued that, without work to occupy the bulk of their waking hours, Americans might find life meaningless. "What we fear to face," writes Professor David Riesman of Harvard, one of the first to raise this issue, "is more than total destruction: it is total meaninglessness."

The fear of dehumanization has been the most pervasive of all, however. One reason for its pervasiveness may be that those who try to dispel the fear have not always done a satisfactory job. The traditional argument is that the impact of technology depends on us—on the purpose to which we put our knowledge, the tasks to which we apply our technology. "We are too prone to make technological instruments the scapegoats for the sins of those who wield them," R.C.A. Chairman David Sarnoff has said. "The products of modern science are not in themselves good or bad; it is the way they are used that determines their value."

In arguing thus, General Sarnoff was following a long and honorable philosophic tradition. "If mankind can rise to the occasion," Alfred North Whitehead wrote some forty years ago, in *Science and the Modern World,* "there lies in front a golden age of beneficent creativeness. But material power in itself is ethically neutral. It can equally well work in the wrong direction." Von Neumann argued in almost identical terms in his 1955 *Fortune* article: "Technology—like science—is neutral all through, providing only means of control applicable to any purpose, indifferent to all."

This view is a half-truth that obscures more than it illuminates. Its proponents are on strong enough ground when they deny that technology *determines* our destinies. The trouble arises when they fail to recognize that technology directly *affects* both the individual and society. For purpose does not exist in a vacuum; men do not choose from an infinite array of alternatives. On the contrary, the alternatives from which they choose are in large part given by their technology; any major advance in science or change in technology throws up new alternatives and erases old ones.

A new technology, moreover, frequently produces unexpected and unintended effects quite independent of its ostensible purpose. Thus the automobile has changed American life—and is now changing life around the globe—in ways that have little to do with the speed at which people drive or their destinations. Both the pattern and the pace of suburbanization, for example, changed drastically in the 1920s, when cars became an item of mass consumption; and dissertations could be—indeed, have been— written on the way the automobile changed sexual behavior. The assembly line, whether it turns out corn flakes or Cadillacs, has had effects far beyond the developers' original purpose, which was simply to reduce production costs; among other things, the assembly line has drastically changed the nature of work, altered the function of management, and reordered the relations among workers and between workers and management.

Some writers, including Daniel Bell, Raymond Aron, and Georges Friedmann, have described the way in which industrialization is imposing a set of "imperatives"—insistent pressures for urbanization, the professionalization of management, the rapid growth of professional and technical employment—that lead to a number of striking similarities in all industrial nations. These pressures operate under both capitalism and socialism, as Bell, for one, has recently argued in a paper on the decline of the Marxist-Leninist ideology in the Soviet Union.

Science and technology alter human purpose in another and more fundamental, if less apparent, way: by affecting our basic and frequently unconscious concepts of the good, the true, and the beautiful. According to Marshall McLuhan, the most stimulating —and controversial—student of technology to have emerged in some years, technology literally changes the way in which we perceive the world. "Like it or not," Richard Schickel wrote in the November 1965 *Harper's,* McLuhan "is on his way to becoming one of those annoying 'seminal' thinkers whose arguments you must adapt, incorporate, or dispose of before pressing ahead in his field."

McLuhan sees each new technology or "medium" as an extension of some part of the human body or capability. For example, the wheel is an extension of the foot, the lever an extension of the arm, tools an extension of the hand. The alphabet and print are extensions of the eye; they translate sounds into sight—i.e., into letters that can be seen on the printed page. "All media are active metaphors in their power to translate experience into new forms."

The extension of any one sense, McLuhan believes, alters the relation among all the senses; it creates a new "sense ratio," a new interplay among the senses. This interplay not only alters concepts of style and content, as the printing press did with literature, but changes the way in which we perceive the world. For perception, as Jerome Bruner and others have demonstrated, is not simply a passive or objective relationship between a viewer and the object being viewed. On the contrary, it is a highly subjective and active process, in which events totally outside the stimulus affect (in some cases determine) what we perceive, and how. As E. H. Gombrich has shown, "the innocent eye sees nothing." We see what we are disposed to see. And what disposes us—what determines the anticipation or expectation that is crucial to perception—is only in small degree biological. It is primarily cultural; we see what our culture (which includes our technology) disposes us to see.

What happens, then, when our culture and technology change? What happens is that we see things we don't now see, and we see familiar things in a very different way, if indeed we see them at all. If the changes are large, a culture's whole perceptual style is likely to change. These changes are most evident in the arts, since the nature of the artist—his function, so to speak—is to be most sensitive to the new "sense ratios or patterns of perception" which new technologies initiate. "Why is it," Gombrich asks in the opening paragraph of his classic *Art and Illusion,* "that different ages and different nations have represented the visible world in such different ways?" The answer is not, as earlier art historians assumed, that techniques improved. "If styles have differed," Gombrich suggests, "it must be because intentions have changed" —because artists in different periods and different nations have perceived "the visible world" in very different ways, reflecting the different technologies and different modes of thought around them. "I think of art, at its most significant," McLuhan argues, "as a DEW line, a Distant Early Warning system that can always be relied on to tell the old culture what is beginning to happen to it."

To say this is not to suggest (as McLuhan frequently seems to) that technology has taken hold and effaced human will, any more than to acknowledge the role and power of the unconscious in individual behavior is to deny the reality of individual choice. It is, rather, to argue that we can enlarge the sphere of choice and use technology to serve human purpose only if we recognize that it affects our purpose, both individually and collectively, and make the effort to understand how. We need to understand what is fixed and what is changeable; in an era of radical change, we particularly need to be able to distinguish the new from the old—the elements of continuity from those of discontinuity. The need, in short, is not for some new "adjustment" to the imperatives of technology; it is for recognition of what those imperatives are, in order that choices may be made and control may be exercised.

Before looking more closely at McLuhan's controversial notions of how technology is changing thought, behavior, and society, it will pay to return to the thesis of Jacques Ellul, whose book, *The Technological Society,* has been enjoying something of a vogue since an English translation was published in this country in 1964. "Just as postwar France established what we call the theatre of the absurd," Arnold Beichman wrote in reviewing the book in the *Christian Science Monitor,* "Professor Ellul may now claim to have produced the sociology of the absurd with his continuing emphasis on man's bewilderment, his helplessness, his utter futility in the world of Technique." What gives Ellul his significance, other reviewers pointed out, is not any special orginality of theme—his thesis has roots in Spengler, Veblen, Huxley, Orwell, Mumford—but rather the systematic, rigorous way in which he presents it and the relentlessness with which he carries it to a logical conclusion—and beyond. *The Technological Society* is the sharpest and least ambiguous of the recent arguments that technology is bringing about a loss of freedom and a subversion of human values. Because of this strong theme—and perhaps also because it had supported American publication of the book—the Center for the Study of Democratic Institutions in December 1965 assembled in Santa Barbara a group of thirty-two scholars, philosophers, and scientists from around the world to discuss Ellul's analysis.

The enemy, according to Ellul, is not the machine; it is not any single technology or group of technologies. It is, rather, what Ellul calls "technique," a concept embracing the machine but going far beyond it. By technique, Ellul principally means the drive to rationalize every human activity, the search for "the one best means in every field"; sometimes, however, he defines technique as "the ensemble of means," i.e., the whole complex of standardized means that have developed. Unfortunately, Ellul is sometimes maddeningly vague about his central concept. His introductory "Note to the Reader" talks of technique as "the totality of methods rationally arrived at and having absolute efficiency (for a given stage of development) in every field of human activity."

What seems to be crucial about technique, however, is its tendency to take over all of man's activities, to "transform everything it touches into a machine." The search for "the one best means" so dominates every activity that this search itself becomes the end; efficiency becomes the purpose of all activity. The end result, Ellul argues, is that "when technique enters into every area of life, including the human, it ceases to be external to man and becomes his very substance." Hence his conclusion that "technique has become autonomous"—that instead of technique serving man, man now serves technique.

Without doubt, Ellul is describing certain clear and disturbing tendencies in contemporary society—tendencies that, if carried to their logical conclusion, would subvert quite a few cherished human values. But is our society's commitment to "the one best means" really so inexorable? Will it—must it—carry that commitment to the extreme foreseen by Ellul?

The answer is no. Certainly Ellul offers no convincing evidence to support his thesis; and many of his arguments are just foolish. Throughout the book, for example, the technique-ridden present is compared with a beautiful, pastoral—and wholly imaginary—past, when man lived in accordance with "the traditional rhythms of life and nature." "Think of our dehumanized factories, our unsatisfied senses, our working women, our estrangement from nature," Ellul demands. But with what shall we contrast this dehumanized world? The beautiful, harmonious life being lived by, say, the Chinese or Vietnamese peasant woman, who works in the fields, close to nature, for twelve hours a day—roughly the conditions under which the great bulk of women (and men) have worked, at least in the temperate zones, through all of human history? For that is the condition that Ellul idealizes. In the Middle Ages, he assures us, "Man sought open spaces, large rooms, the possibility of moving about, of seeing beyond his nose, of not constantly colliding with other people." This would have been startling news to the medieval peasant, who lived with his wife and children, other relatives, and probably animals as well in a one-room thatched cottage. And even for the nobility, was there really more "possibility of moving about" in the Middle Ages, when travel was by foot or hoof, than today, when steelworkers spend their sabbaticals in Europe?

MacArthur and the raincoats

Ellul's pages are filled with this sort of doubtful history. "Consider . . . our hospitals," he pleads, "in which [man] is only a number"—but in which, one has to add, the chances of his becoming well are quite a lot better than they were in any hospital in the harmonious past. Shall we contrast the dehumanizing medical care of our time with, say, that of the idyllic fourteenth century, when man lived in harmony with the rhythms of nature—and perhaps half the population of England died in just two years as a result of the Black Death?

When he writes of technique's tendency to take over, to subordinate ends to means, Ellul is often equally silly:

The politician, he tells us, "no longer has any real choice; decision follows automatically from the preparatory technical labors." The evidence? In the United States, we are informed, on the authority of a German writer, "unchallengeable decisions have already been made by 'electronic brains' in the service of the National Bureau of Standards; for example, by the EAC, surnamed the 'Washington Oracle.' The EAC is said to have been the machine which made the decision to recall General MacArthur after it had solved equations containing all the strategic and economic variables of his plan." The fact, of course, is that Harry S. Truman made the decision. The Bureau of Standards did then have a computer (its correct name was SEAC), which did make some decisions for the Pentagon—for example, how many Army raincoats to order, and in what sizes.

Technique, Ellul asserts, "possesses monopoly of action. No human activity is possible except as it is mediated and censored by the technical medium. . . . Not even the simplest initiative can have an original, independent existence."

The evidence? "Suppose one were to write a revolutionary book," Ellul explains. "If it is to be published, it must enter into the framework of the technical organization of book publishing. In a predominantly capitalistic technical culture, the book can be published only if it can return a profit. Thus, it must appeal to some public and hence must refrain from attacking the real taboos of the public for which it is destined"—a statement that will come as news to such angry social critics as Paul Goodman and Norman Mailer. "Any author who seeks to have his manuscript published must make it conform to certain lines laid down by the potential publishers," Ellul goes on the explain. Thus, "the bourgeois publishing house will not publish Lenin; the 'revolutionary' publishing house will not publish Paul Bourget; and no one will publish a book attacking the real religion of our times, by which I mean the dominant social forces of the technological society." As the English philosopher J. P. Corbett of the University of Sussex sardonically asked in a critique of Ellul, "What more need be said about Professor Ellul's methods of handling evidence, except to wonder whether he had much difficulty in getting *his* book published?"

Ellul's conspiratorial view of events rushing headlong toward the Apocalypse may be taken as a prime example of what the historian Richard Hofstadter calls "the paranoid style"—a kind of literature to which Americans seem addicted. (Other recent examples include Rachel Carson's *Silent Spring,* Vance Packard's *The Hidden Persuaders,* and Paul Goodman's *Growing Up Absurd.*) This approach to the contemporary scene, Professor Corbett says, involves "taking hold of some social phenomenon or other, describing it with an impressive array of pejorative terms, illustrating it by a series of spine-chilling examples, making the reader feel, like the reader of a good ghost story, that all his ordinary assumptions are in jeopardy, but then leaving him with the impression that nothing whatever can be done, whether in theory or in practice, to put things right." The appeal is understandably great. "You thus get all the thrills of virtue with all the comforts of inaction; you are taken to the brink of destiny only to find yourself tucked up snugly in the electric blanket of existing institutions; your guilty conscience is given a salubrious airing, and yet everything is allowed to go on precisely as before."

A message about media

What distinguishes Marshall McLuhan from most other grand theorists of the technological society is his avoidance of the paranoid style. For McLuhan joyously welcomes the technological and cultural changes that other writers fear or criticize, and he has succeeded in changing the terms of the debate over what is happening to man in this era of radical change. "Other observers," the art critic Harold Rosenberg wrote in reviewing McLuhan's *Understanding Media* for *The New Yorker,* "have been content to repeat criticisms of industrial society that were formulated a century ago, as if civilization had been steadily emptied out since the advent of the power loom. As against the images of our time as a faded photograph of a richly pigmented past, McLuhan, for all his abstractness, has found positive, humanistic meaning and the color of life in supermarkets, stratospheric flight, the lights blinking on broadcasting towers." Looking at the same phenomena that Ellul and others see as dehumanizing man, McLuhan "has dared to seek the cure in the disease, and his vision of going forward into primitive wholeness is a good enough reply to those who would go back to it." Indeed, McLuhan's work is a "concrete testimonial" to the conviction "that man is certain to find his footing in the new world he is in the process of creating."

McLuhan's ideas about what is happening now can be understood best in relation to his ideas about technology's past impact on human society, particularly in the past several hundred years. The theory is summed up in McLuhan's epigram, "The medium is the message," by which he means that *societies are shaped more by the nature of the media through which men communicate than by the content of their communications.* In its most general form, as originally developed, for example, by the historian Harold Innis, on whom McLuhan relies very heavily, this idea is less paradoxical or controversial than it sounds. It is now widely believed, for example, that the inventions of hand tools and spoken language are what differentiated man from the beasts, enabling him to create social systems of an elaborateness and duration unknown among any other species. Just when or how this happened is shrouded in mystery. But most students of evolution now believe that it was the development of tools and of language that led to the development of the human brain and its differentiation from the brain of any other species—rather than the other way around.

The next great "technological" development, in McLuhan's view, was the invention of writing—a clear example of the "medium" being more important than the "message." For once men start to write, they become conscious of time in a way never possible before; writing enormously enlarges society's collective memory, and so social organization begins to extend backward into the past and forward into the future in a way impossible in a preliterate society. More important, perhaps, writing also leads to the breakup of tribal society and the emergence of individualism in the Western sense—the phenomenon nineteenth-century English historians referred to as the shift from "status" to "contract."

The point is that individualism is virtually a byproduct of literacy. Preliterate societies are oral societies; they live in a world of sound. Whereas for us "seeing is believing," for the preliterate hearing is believing; reality resides in what is heard and said. Because oral communication requires proximity, oral societies tend to be collective. As David Riesman has put it, "When a whole society depends on what individuals can remember, it can hardly help depending on every device of the demagogue and the poet: rhyme, rhythm, melody, structure, repetition." Since people "tend to remember best the things they have felt most deeply," the memorable words in an oral culture will tend to be "those most charged with group feeling"; communication will "keep alive in an individual the childhood sense of dependence, childhood's terrors and elations, and something of its awe for the old." Indeed, "one can hardly speak of *individuals* in the modern sense in such cultures."

The gunpowder of the mind

Once books enter the environment, it can never be the same again; in Riesman's phrase, books are "the gunpowder of the mind." They "bring with them detachment and a critical attitude that is not possible in oral tradition. . . . If oral communication keeps people together, print is the isolating medium par excellence." For the invention of writing, as Professor Kenneth Boulding writes, "made it possible for the present to speak to the future and to hear from the past. It also made it possible for one man to communicate with people far beyond the range of his voice." In McLuhan's phrase, the book substitutes the eye for the ear; this substitution causes "the most radical explosion that can occur in any culture."

In the West the explosion occurred in two stages, widely separated over time. The first was the development of the phonetic alphabet, which transformed Greek life in the sixth and fifth centuries B.C. and laid the groundwork for what we consider Western civilization. Socrates was the last great product—and champion—of the oral tradition. Plato used the new medium of prose (poetry had been the medium before, since it is easier to remember than prose) to record Socrates' conversation—an attempt to preserve the power of the spoken word on the written page.* With Aristotle, the world passed from exclusive reliance on oral instruction to the new habit of reading. Even so, the oral tradition remained very strong until the invention of the printing press in the fifteenth century.

It was this invention and its after effects—what McLuhan calls "The Gutenberg Galaxy"—that completed the "detribalization of Western man." For printing enormously amplified the effects of the written word. The effects were not just quantitative, however; the printing press did not simply mean more of the same. For print, unlike manuscript, is uniform and endlessly repeatable. The printed book "was the first teaching machine," McLuhan writes. "By putting the same text in front of any given number of stu-

* The dialogues show that Socrates and Plato were as contemptuous of the new medium of their day as literary critics like Dwight MacDonald are of our new media. "The discovery of the alphabet," Socrates argues in the *Phaedrus*, "will create forgetfulness in the learners' souls, because they will not use their memories; they will trust to the external written characters and not remember of themselves . . . You give your disciples not truth, but only the semblance of truth; they will be hearers of many things, and will have learned nothing; they will appear to be omniscient and will generally know nothing."

dents or readers, print ended the scholastic regime of oral disputation very quickly." The Elluls of that period were convinced, of course, that the printing press would bring about the dehumanization of the individual.

The result was precisely the opposite—the flowering of the individual. For the portability of the book allowed "typographic man" to learn by himself, thus encouraging individualism, as well as the peculiarly modern distinction (first celebrated in *Hamlet*) between knowing and doing. And the repetitiveness of print, by permitting the almost endless multiplication of messages, carried men away from the intimate, complex—and confining—relationships of what was still a predominantly tribal society. Together with the emphasis on linear sequence and continuity, this made possible the development of large-scale organization and of abstract human relationships. Hence print, as Kenneth Boulding writes in summarizing McLuhan's thesis, led Western man "from tribalism into nationhood, from feudalism into capitalism, from craftsmanship into mass production, from lore into science."

Life in the global village

Now, McLuhan argues, all this is being reversed; the history of the past 400 years—in a sense, of the past 2,500 years—is being played backward. Print produced an "explosion" that shattered tribal unity and broke society up into separate elements. Electric and electronic technology—television, radio, the telephone, the computer—is causing what he insists on calling an "implosion," forcing people back together in tribal unity, albeit on a global scale, returning us to the world of the oral and the simultaneous, the world of emotion and sensory expression.

For one thing, the ear is becoming much more important. People are again getting information by hearing it—over the telephone, the radio, and increasingly via television, which McLuhan considers an aural rather than a visual medium. Here again, his ideas in their more generalized forms have considerable scholarly support. It is widely agreed that, even apart from new media, more and more of today's communication is verbal in the traditional face-to-face sense. "Everything is moving so fast," says geneticist Ruth Sager of Columbia University, "that most important scientific communication is verbal. Things do get published in journals, of course, but that's for documentation." The new communication media, moreover, extend man's ear around the globe the way the book extended his vision.

Oral communication, we have seen, immerses the individual in the group, involves him (to use a favorite McLuhan term) in the feelings and affairs of others. The speed of electric and electronic circuitry substitute the simultaneous for the sequential, ending both time and space as we have known them for the past several centuries. Thus contemporary man, peering into his television screen, is in much the same position as preliterate or tribal man; he is forming his view of the world through direct, firsthand observation, the only difference being that his village is the whole world. As with his tribal ancestor, "action and reaction occur almost at the same time."

Television heightens the need of, and the search for, involvement in several other ways. The most important arises out of the fact that it provides what engineers call a "low-definition image." Compared to a photograph, for example, television provides relatively little information per square inch. A sixteen-inch-square photograph can show several dozen people clearly and sharply; if you try to show that many people on a TV screen, it comes out as one big blur. The result is that television, to use the language of gestalt psychology, provides an "incomplete loop"; the viewer feels the need to complete the loop himself.

Ours is the first society in history, McLuhan believes, to have the opportunity to escape technological determinism: this belief is the major source of his optimism.* "Hitherto most people have accepted their cultures as a fate, like climate or vernacular," McLuhan argued in *The Gutenberg Galaxy* (a much better and more convincing book than his more recent *Understanding Media*). We can free ourselves from fate, however, for "we can transcend the limitations of our own assumptions by a critique of

---

* It's not the only source. McLuhan is nothing if not contradictory, and he frequently seems to be saying that technological determinism is inescapable—but that the culture being produced by the new technology is superior to the old.

them. We can now live, not just amphibiously in divided and distinguished worlds, but pluralistically in many worlds and cultures simultaneously. We are no more committed to one culture— to a single ratio among the human senses—than to one book or to one language or to one technology." But freedom of choice, McLuhan warns, depends on making the effort to understand the process by which technology affects our culture. "Our need today is, culturally, the same as the scientist's who seeks to become aware of the bias of the instruments of research in order to correct that bias."

What makes McLuhan one of the major intellectual influences of our time is the fact that he is one of the few people making the effort to understand how technology really is affecting us. His attempt to fit miscellaneous phenomena, from the Beatles to false eyelashes to pop art, into his grand scheme of things can be exasperating; but this same attempt to discover the meaning of the commonplace provides occasional blinding flashes of illumination.

Against this achievement, the question of whether McLuhan is right or wrong in his specific interpretation of current technological change is relatively unimportant, if not irrelevant. As Kenneth Boulding puts it, "It is perhaps typical of very creative minds that they hit very large nails not quite on the head." For all its faults, McLuhan's work offers one possible answer to those looking for encouragement about man's ability to survive.

Greek scholars and boxers

Certainly there is another possible answer, however. The answer may begin by observing that the question has been asked before, and answered in the affirmative. "From the dawn of history," Whitehead wrote in *Science and the Modern World,* in many ways still the best treatment of the impact of science, "mankind has always been losing its religious faith, has always suffered from the malignant use of material power, has always suffered from the infertility of its best intellectual types, has always witnessed the periodical decadence of art." And yet, Whitehead argues, "mankind has progressed. Even if you take a tiny oasis of peculiar excellence, the type of modern man who would have most chance of happiness in ancient Greece at its best period is probably (as now) an average professional heavyweight boxer, and not an average Greek scholar from Oxford or Germany. Indeed, the main use of the Oxford scholar would have been his capability of writing an ode in glorification of the boxer. Nothing does more harm in unnerving men for their duties in the present than the attention devoted to the points of excellence in the past as compared with the average failure of the present day."

And yet complacency about the impact of science and technology is hardly in order. There have been periods of decadence and destruction in the past. And our age *is* different, in ways we do not, as yet, fully understand; we are living in an era of radical change. One critical difference about our age, according to Emmanuel G. Mesthene, executive director of the Harvard University Program on Technology and Society, is that modern technology puts the traditional problems of choice in a totally different context. Until the present, Professor Mesthene argues, the arena of human action was limited by the state of the physical world. Politics, for example, was carried on within the context of weapons of a certain power and mobility, of oceans and mountains of a given width and height, of weather that could be neither controlled nor predicted, of communication and transportation networks of given speeds and capacities. "Of course, weapons, and speeds, and technologies all changed over time. Even mountains did." But the changes occurred so slowly that they were seen, if indeed they were seen at all, as effects, after they had occurred. For practical purposes, the physical and technological constraints were fixed and certain. "The decision-maker couldn't change them, just as the baseball manager can't move the short left-field fence when the star right-hander of the opposing team comes to bat." Hence the role of thought was to distinguish what was possible from what was not. And the question of choice—"Can we do this?"—meant, in practice, "Do the rules allow it?"

The movable left-field fence

The critical characteristic of today's technology, Mesthene argues, is the way it has collapsed the old time span. By shortening the process of change, technology is shifting the way in which the question of choice is formulated. "Can we do this?" no longer means "Can we do this within the rules?" but rather, "Can we change the rules?" Frequently—more frequently than McLuhan or Mesthene supposes—the answer is no. But certainly there are times when it is yes—when the old physical and technological constraints no longer hold. Both radar and the atom bomb, which affected the course of World War II, were developed during that war. Similarly, new devices to detect underground nuclear explosions were developed while the arms-control talks were going on, and they affected the outcome of those talks. As Mesthene puts it, "It is now possible, for the first time ever, to move the left-field fence *during* the game."

The result is to enlarge rather than to restrict the sphere of human action and choice—to make it possible, if you will, for steelworkers to vacation in Europe or Hawaii, or even Miami Beach. It is also to create new dangers—which is something *not* new. "It is the business of the future to be dangerous," Whitehead wrote, adding, "In the immediate future there will be less security than in the immediate past, less stability. It must be admitted that there is a degree of instability which is inconsistent with civilization. But, on the whole, the great ages have been unstable ages."

Chart 9. Average Ann
Greater Prod

5

4

3

2

1

0

Percent

1947-57

Employers can increase
workers and by using
ductivity, or output per
important for output ga
1957, for example, real
product in constant do
ductivity gains account
1957-60, a period of
accounted for all the e
gross private product g
productivity has accoun
the gains in employment

that fantastic gain of
a shortage of men or
for employers to cont
    Aside from the bu
no question is more in

7

Business Can Live
with the "Labor Shortage"

"THE GROWTH OF REAL OUTPUT," Gardner Ackley, chairman of the Council of Economic Advisers, told a meeting of economists in December 1965, "cannot forever be as fast as we have had during the past several years." His reason was simple: "At some point, the economy will really be operating at the ceiling set by labor-force growth and the advance of productivity." Ackley's proposition was unarguable; indeed, it was hardly more than a truism. Just a few months after Ackley made the point, however, it had come to seem a lot less academic. By the spring of 1966, unemployment was no longer a problem, except for specific groups, such as Negro men and Negro teenagers, and people had stopped worrying that productivity was growing too fast. On the contrary, both businessmen and government officials had become very much concerned about labor shortages and, related to the shortages, about the difficulty of maintaining the productivity standards of recent years.

Those standards have been high. Labor productivity—i.e., output per man-hour—has increased by more than 20 percent in the five years since the great boom got under way. It was this rise, combined with a 10 percent rise in employment, that produced

Chart 9. Average Annual Increase in Output Attributable to Greater Productivity and Higher Employment

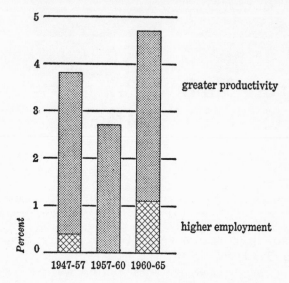

greater productivity

higher employment

Percent

1947-57 1957-60 1960-65

Employers can increase output in two principal ways: by hiring more workers and by using workers more efficiently—i.e., increasing productivity, or output per man-hour. Productivity has been far more important for output gains in the postwar years. Between 1947 and 1957, for example, real output in the private economy (gross private product in constant dollars) increased 3.8 percent a year and productivity gains accounted for nearly 90 percent of this increase. In 1957–60, a period of slower economic growth, productivity gains accounted for all the expansion in output. Between 1960 and 1965 gross private product grew by an impressive 4.7 percent a year and productivity has accounted for three-quarters of this growth. However, the gains in employment have been sharp, too.

that fantastic gain of one-third in real gross national product. Will a shortage of men or a lag in productivity now make it impossible for employers to continue expanding output in line with demand?

Aside from the budget uncertainties stemming from Vietnam, no question is more important for the course of the economy over the near and intermediate term. The question really involves two others: (1) By how much can man-hours be increased, either by employing more people or by lengthening hours worked? (2) How much is productivity likely to increase?

The answers are more optimistic than most current discussion assumes. To be sure, it's getting harder to find new employees, and the employees are likely to be less experienced, less educated, and less motivated—hence less productive—than those generally hired in recent years. But the United States does not yet face a labor shortage in any absolute sense; employment and productivity are still growing, and can continue to grow, provided only that business identifies its new problems correctly and responds to them intelligently and creatively.

Many businessmen will find this statement hard to accept. "This is the worst manpower shortage I've ever seen—worse than during the Korean war, worse even than World War II," says John Bailer, manufacturing manager of the Miehle Co. of Chicago, a division of Miehle-Goss-Dexter, a major producer of printing presses. Bailer's evaluation of the current labor situation is widely shared, especially in the Great Lakes area, where businessmen complain about scraping the bottom of the barrel. "If I wanted to hire bodies, I could," the personnel manager of one large plant put it, "but I can't find anyone I can use."

The problem is real; it would be naive to suggest that the pool of labor available has the same quality it had when the unemployment rate was nearly 7 percent. Some perspective on the new labor market may be gained by considering the three stages that business has gone through in expanding production and employment.

When the boom got under way in the first quarter of 1961, nearly five million people—6.8 percent of the labor force—were unemployed. The great bulk of them, some 85 percent, were experienced workers. Another three million (half of them people who normally worked full time) were partially unemployed; they were working part time only because they could not find full-time jobs. Thus as business expanded output, it was at first able to meet its manpower needs without any difficulty. Experienced workers were available for skilled and unskilled jobs alike.

In the second stage, as the reservoir of available experienced workers diminished, employers had to turn more frequently to younger or less experienced people—teenagers, young adults, married women. But they were still able to maintain extraordinarily high hiring standards, e.g., by refusing to interview anyone without a high school diploma. As a result, they had no difficulty hiring workers who could be trained quickly and easily to do the jobs for which they were hired, and who, in addition, had the capacity (and the ambition) to move into more responsible or more highly skilled jobs later on.

The tight third stage

During the fall and winter of 1965–66, in the third stage of the expansion, the unemployment rate for the labor force as a whole dropped below 4.5 percent. The rate for married men fell below 2.5 percent and then below 2 percent, and employers began having more and more trouble finding the high-quality people they were used to. Hence the widespread feeling that they were close to the bottom of the barrel.

As the labor market continues to tighten, employers' ability to hire additional workers will depend more and more on the speed and imagination with which they adjust to the new conditions of supply—on their willingness to adjust hiring procedures and standards, alter job descriptions and work arrangements, provide better training and supervision, etc. There is every incentive for them to do so; the prolongation of the boom and the expansion of the war in Vietnam have brought to a head a number of changes in the labor market that would have arrived soon anyway—changes that employers will have to live with for a long time. And making such adjustments will be nothing new. Again and again in the past, United States business has shown a remarkable capacity to use whatever supply of labor happened to be available, changing the people to fit the job requirements and changing the job requirements to fit the people. Business did it during World War II, when sharecroppers were turned into shipbuilders, domestics into riveters, overnight; did it again during the Korean war; and is likely to do it—indeed, is already doing it—this time.

Reaching down the line

But do the unemployed or, for that matter, the people now entering the labor force, really have the education, skill, experience, and motivation that employers need? To begin with, the unemployed *always* appear to be workers of dubious quality; to be unemployed means, by definition, to be marginal to the state of demand that happens to exist at the moment. For the labor market is a kind of giant shape-up, with members of the labor force lined up in order of their relative attractiveness to employers. And to the extent that the market operates efficiently, employers start at the head of the line, selecting as many as they need of the workers most attractive to them, the number depending on the general state of the economy. As demand rises, employers always have to reach farther down the line to find additional help.

Thus quality is a relative as much as an absolute concept. And the Labor Department's surveys of the characteristics of the unemployed suggest that, even on an absolute basis, employers haven't reached the bottom of the barrel yet. Relatively few of the unemployed, to be sure, can meet the requirements for professional, technical, or highly skilled jobs, but they are certainly not unemployable. Of the 3,000,000 people who were unemployed in March 1966, for example, 2,400,000 were seeking full-time jobs, and all but 200,000 of these had previous full-time work experience. For most, the work experience was recent; half had been out of work only a month or less. No more than one in ten could be considered hard-core unemployed or unemployable; this was the number that had been out of work for six months or longer.

More to the point, perhaps, neither the existing array of job requirements named by employers nor the array of job skills possessed by the labor force is immutable. On the contrary, both tend to change with great speed when the state of the market dictates. "It is the proper function of a market to allocate resources," the National Commission on Technology, Automation, and Economic Progress pointed out in discussing this question in its report to the President, "and in this respect the labor market does not function differently from any other. If the available resources are of high quality, the market will adjust to the use of high-quality resources; if the quality is low, methods will be developed to use such resources." Japan and Western Europe, the report observed, operate sophisticated industrial economies with labor forces whose educational level is far below our own.

At least part of the reason businessmen are grumbling about scraping the bottom of the barrel, therefore, is that they were "spoiled" by eight years of a loose labor market. Because they were able to hire experienced craftsmen to fill any vacancies that occurred, companies did not bother to train their own future supply. Sometimes, it should be added, companies that *did* want to train more craftsmen were discouraged by unions anxious to hold down the supply of skilled men. Even for the less skilled jobs, more and more corporations made high school graduation a prerequisite for employment. This tendency was also exaggerated by trade-union contractual requirements that companies promote from within, in accordance with fairly rigid seniority provisions and other union restrictions on management's freedom to lay men off or reassign them to other jobs. These provisions became more confining in recent years. Concerned about high unemployment and convinced that automation was destroying jobs, the unions adopted a strategy they now deeply regret: in effect, they traded wage increases for greater job security or for earlier retirement. (See Chapter 4.) The stability in unit labor costs during the first four years of the expansion was due more to this union strategy and to the looseness of the labor market than to the Administration's guideposts.

By and large, employers' complaints about a shortage of labor reflect their own lag in adjusting to new conditions in the labor market as much as an inability to find people. Where there is a labor shortage, that is to say, it is at least partly self-imposed—the result of hiring standards that exclude the people now available.

A special task force from the departments of Labor and Commerce that studied the employment situation in Milwaukee in December 1965 reached much the same conclusion. Milwaukee businessmen did their share of grumbling about the difficulty of finding adequate help. But where companies had trouble meeting production schedules, it was because of a shortage of materials or

Chart 10. Labor Costs: The New Equation

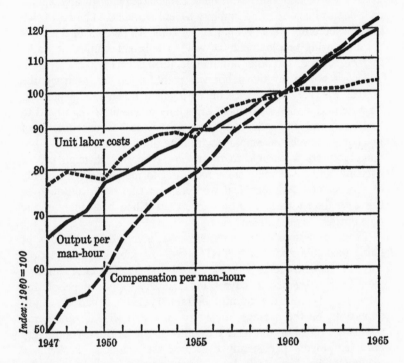

During most of the postwar years, productivity was not rising as fast as workers' compensation; hence the rise in unit labor costs. These have been relatively stable since 1960, as productivity kept pace with compensation. In 1960–65 productivity in the private economy—gross private product per man-hour—increased by an average of 3.6 percent a year, a rate well above the 3.2 percent average for the 1947–60 period. Hourly compensation (including fringe benefits) was slowing down, meanwhile; the gain averaged 4.2 percent a year in 1960–65, versus 5.4 percent in 1947–60. Union policy contributed to the slowdown; persuaded that automation was destroying jobs, many unions pushed for job security rather than higher wages.

This stability in unit labor costs is proving hard to maintain, however. With unemployment below 4 percent, the pressure on wages is increasing. The pressure on employers to hire less efficient men is also likely to hold productivity gains below the average of the past five years. The 1965 increase was down to 2.8 percent.

plant capacity; the task force could find no companies that had lost production or had had to cut back expansion plans to any significant degree because of an inability to find workers. (The task force interviewed employers accounting for some 40 percent of the city's manufacturing employment, as well as a broad sample of trade, finance, service, and other nonmanufacturing firms.)

This is not to say that labor was plentiful; on the contrary, the market was very tight, with unemployment down to 2.3 percent. Experienced skilled craftsmen, especially machinists, were hard to find—in good part, the task force found, as "a consequence of inadequate levels of employer training in previous years"—but manufacturers were able to meet their schedules through use of overtime and by farming some work out to job shops. The supply of professional and technical workers was also tight, although in this case the shortage was no worse than it had been most of the time during the past fifteen years.

The most serious complaints, however, involved the difficulty of filling unskilled and "entry-level" jobs—the jobs in which people enter the labor force as janitors, office boys, etc. The U.S. Employment Service seemed to have a fairly steady supply of people for these jobs (across the country in January 1966 it had three job applicants, on the average, for every job listed with it) and some companies relied on the service to fill their needs. But a good many other employers persistently described the available workers as unemployable. The task force disagreed; in its judgment, the problem was less unemployability than inflexibility on the part of the employers. "Milwaukee employers have traditionally been able to hire workers from the open market who already had the requisite skills," the task force reported to Secretary of Labor Willard Wirtz, "and hence the current group of new, inexperienced, and untrained workers is something that they are not able fully to understand or utilize." In particular, the task force found Milwaukee employers were not making adequate use of Negroes.

The boom in teenage employment

The best reason for thinking that firms *can* use the supply of labor that is available is that so many already have. Consider, for example, the enormous rise that has taken place in employment of teenagers. In the spring of 1965 there were warnings on all sides of a dire and rapidly worsening crisis of teenage unemployment. One expert on youth employment estimated that some 250,000 entry jobs were disappearing each year as a result of technological change, and Secretary Wirtz solemnly announced that "a person needs fourteen years of education to compete with machines." (See Chapter 3.) With a record number of teenagers—some high school graduates, some dropouts—scheduled to enter the labor market, the outlook did look grim indeed. What in fact happened confounded the most soaring optimist: *teenage employment increased as much between January 1965 and January 1966 as it had in the entire ten years preceding.* In those twelve months, teenage employment went up by 1,100,000 (from 4,600,000 to 5,700,000), accounting for fully half the total rise in employment, although teenagers constitute only 8 percent of the employed labor force. The rise in teenage employment, moreover, exceeded the predicted growth in the teenage labor force, as the proportion of fourteen- to seventeen-year-olds seeking work rose sharply, reversing a ten-year decline. Employers hired teenagers for both full-time and part-time jobs, the former increasing 28 percent, the latter 21 percent. The kinds of jobs they obtained changed too; many boys who normally would have started their working lives as laborers found skilled or semiskilled jobs last year. Nearly half the rise in employment of teenage boys, in fact, was in semiskilled or skilled blue-collar occupations; by contrast, the number working as laborers was unchanged.

As the reserve supply of able-bodied adult males has diminished, moreover, employers have started to use women for a great many jobs normally done by men. The increase in female employment during 1965 ran 500,000 above the normal increase in the labor force, with some of the gain registered in the number of female blue-collar workers in durable-goods industries, which normally employ only male production workers. Employers will turn to women workers more and more, for the supply is quite elastic, increasing or decreasing in response to the number of available jobs. Married women with older children are particularly apt to move in and out of the labor force, looking for temporary jobs when they need money for a new refrigerator or the down payment on a new car. When pay is good and jobs are plentiful, many such women can be persuaded to stay in the labor force the year round; for a good many, the availability of a job near home, or with hours conforming to the household schedule, can mean the difference between working and being out of the labor force.

Where the girls are

Companies are using a variety of devices to draw more women into the labor force. The Bank of America, for example, tries to keep in touch with women employees who leave to get married or have a child, in the hope of bringing them back at a later date—if not full time, then to a part-time job, filling in at peak hours.

R.C.A., whose labor needs are enormous because of booming color-television sales, is also going where the girls are. (In its radio and TV assembly plants, women normally constitute two-thirds of the labor force.) Despite an unemployment rate of 2 percent or less in Indianapolis, the company is building a new $14-million assembly plant in Wayne Township, just outside the city, that will employ several thousand. In the suburbs and on the farms in the area, R.C.A. believes, are many women who can be attracted to work at a new factory—some of them, in the opinion of R.C.A. personnel men, from as far away as eighty miles. Meanwhile, 400 miles to the south, in Memphis, R.C.A. is building an even larger plant. "Memphis is an under-industrialized city with an abundant supply of people in the categories we need," Frank McClure, an R.C.A. personnel vice president, explains. "Firestone and International Harvester are there, but they employ mostly males; we expect to hire their wives and daughters."

To find the *males* it needs to expand manufacture of color-television tubes, R.C.A. is building a $26-million factory in Scranton, Pennsylvania, which still has a large pool—6.4 percent—of unemployed. (The city is one of nineteen still classified as having "substantial unemployment.") In the twelve months before R.C.A. decided on Scranton, the employment service there had received 8,000 job applications from people under the age of twenty-two. Another employer tested the labor marked in Scranton by running an ad announcing that a large (unnamed) company was moving to the area and needed workers. Some 14,000 people returned the coupon in the ad, and 10,000 of them completed formal job applications—still without knowing the name of the employer. (The company hired about 400.)

Other companies are trying to tap the remaining "labor surplus" areas by urging unemployed or underemployed men and women to move where the work is. General Motors, for example, is trying to get able-bodied men in West Virginia and Kentucky to move to Detroit, where the labor market is tight. (In Lordstown, Ohio, incidentally, just outside Youngstown, G.M. was flooded with 35,000 applications for work in a new plant in which it expects to employ 5,700.) U.S. Steel has been trying to persuade steel-workers in Pittsburgh to move to Gary, Indiana. Other companies are recruiting workers or building plants in Arkansas and Tennessee, where the small towns still have a large labor supply. Some are scouring the woods of northern New England, Michigan, and Minnesota, luring farmers and independent farmer loggers to factory jobs.

Sometimes the surplus workers are close at hand—but still hard to get at. In Chicago, Oakland, and Los Angeles there are large pools of unemployed Negroes living in the central city, while factories outside the city limits are short of unskilled and semi-skilled men. In part, the problem is that the Negroes living downtown simply have no way to get to the factories. Inland Steel is quite unprejudiced in its hiring, but Negroes living on Chicago's South Side still find it hard to work there because they lack cars and there is virtually no public transportation available. There are similar problems in getting to the U.S. Steel, National Steel, and Bethlehem plants around Chicago.

From shoe salesman to "roller"

To use the supply of labor that happens to be available now—women, teenagers, young adults, Negroes—companies may have to provide considerably more training and supervision than they have previously. But there is evidence that skills can be taught and experience can be acquired in remarkably short periods of time, when the pressure on management is great enough.

Bethlehem Steel's huge new steel-finishing plant at Burns Harbor, Indiana, thirty miles outside Chicago, is a case in point. Construction of the $400-million plant—according to Bethlehem, it is the largest privately financed construction project in the world—began early in 1963. The first unit, a 720,000-ton plate mill, began operations on November 30, 1964, when the labor market in the Chicago area had already begun to tighten. Since then, a cold-rolled sheet mill and a tinplate mill have been opened. Employment ran to around 2,000 in the spring of 1966 and was expected to jump to 2,500 later in the year, when a hot-rolled sheet mill starts operations.

Virtually the entire Burns Harbor labor force was "manufactured" on the site by Bethlehem, to its own specifications. Except for management and supervisory personnel, none of the employees were transferred from other Bethlehem plants; very few of them were steelworkers by trade, and many had never been inside a factory before. The company devised and conducted its own training courses, run by foremen transferred from Bethlehem, Pennsylvania, and Sparrows Point, Maryland. Under pressure, the traditional training times were cut drastically. For example, "rollers," the top skill in a plate mill, were trained in two months, whereas the industry had always allotted at least forty-nine months for training plate-mill rollers. And what kind of men were trained to be rollers in just two months? One had been operating a farm thirty miles away; another had been drifting from job to job for ten or twelve years as a vacuum-cleaner salesman, shoe salesman, construction worker, etc. Most were quite young and youthful exuberance has created some problems—e.g., two brief wildcat strikes. "They take this more as a pep rally than a line of work," a Burns Harbor official says. Even so, Bethlehem is well pleased: "The kids have done a real fine job—much better than we expected." And, in fact, the plate mill—the only unit that is completely shaken down—is outperforming the engineers' expectations.

Training has its limits, of course; for some jobs, particularly professional or technical jobs, training takes too long or presupposes more intelligence, education, and aptitude than the people available possess. But in these cases employers can often solve the problem in other ways. One way is to hire moonlighters; a midwestern metalworking firm has set up a special five-hour evening shift specifically designed to attract moonlighters. Another is to upgrade employees already on the payroll, hiring new applicants to fill the unskilled or semiskilled jobs that are vacated as a result. In 1965, for example, employment of skilled workers went up by 235,000. Since the number who were unemployed declined by only 49,000, and since formal apprenticeship programs graduated only a handful, employers obviously met the bulk of their needs by upgrading employees. The most fruitful approach is to redesign the job itself. A fairly chronic shortage of mechanical draftsmen, nurses, and social workers, for example, is being met by changes in organization; the changes permit "sub-professonal" personnel to handle many of the routine or menial tasks that have traditionally been part of these occupations, thereby freeing the professionals to do the things only they can do. Manufacturers, especially in the metalworking industries, are now using some such approach to relieve the shortage of machinists. The process is often referred to as "work simplification" or "job dilution."

The colleges and the draft

In any case, it is a fact that nonfarm employers were able to add 925,000 workers to their payrolls in the first three months of 1966, a rate of increase below that of the preceding quarter but substantially above that of the preceding year. They were able to do this, moreover, without any evident worsening of the spot shortages and imbalances that had existed for some time, and without any unusual pressure on wage rates. Average hourly earnings of factory workers were $2.68 in March 1966, versus $2.66 in December and $2.59 in March 1965. The employment service continued to have three applicants for every job listed with it.

In all probability, employers will continue to be able to meet their employment needs. The labor force is still growing very rapidly (though nearly everybody has stopped worrying that it is growing *too* fast). The Bureau of Labor Statistics projects an annual increase in the labor force during the second half of this decade some 50 percent greater, on the average, than the increases of the 1960–65 period, and nearly twice that of the 1950s. For 1966—i.e., from December 1965 to December 1966—a "normal" increase (one in line with long-term trends) would be 1,300,000, or 1.6 percent.

To some extent, of course, the increase in the *civilian* labor force will be held down by the buildup of the armed forces. The growth of the labor force has also been held down recently by the extraordinary increase in college attendance. In part, at least, these attendance figures reflect a desire to avoid the draft (fewer upperclassmen are dropping out). Should draft calls be stepped up substantially, however, the standards for deferment will be made more stringent. To a considerable extent, therefore, increased draft calls would affect the number of college students rather than the labor force; and besides, any step-up in the draft would induce many a student to abandon college for a job in a defense plant, where the chances of deferment would be greater. On balance, and barring a buildup considerably beyond 400,000 troops in Vietnam, which would require calling up the reserves, the draft and the colleges are not likely to cut the expected labor-force growth by more than 300,000 or 400,000.

In any case, young men of draft age represent only a small part of the normal increase in the labor force; any reduction in their number is likely to be offset, or more than offset, by abnormal increases in a number of other categories. The strong demand for labor is likely to pull into the labor market a great many women and some older men who might not otherwise be looking for work; it may also draw into full-time jobs a great many men and women who normally work only part time or for part of the year. Many men who might have retired may remain in the labor force to take advantage of higher wages and overtime pay; and some who have already retired may even be induced to return to work. Taking everything together, it seems reasonable to expect the civilian labor force to grow by 1,200,000, and perhaps by as much as 1,500,000 —i.e., at about the normal rate.

The "frictional" rate

Employment might increase even more rapidly than the labor force, for there is still that reservoir of unemployed people—as of March 1966, there were three million, or 3.8 percent of the labor force. Not all the unemployed can be put to work, of course; a certain number will always be out of work because employers fire inefficient or insubordinate or unneeded workers, and employees quit and turn down unsatisfactory job offers. No one really knows how low this "frictional unemployment" can get. It depends in part on how quickly workers looking for jobs get into contact with employers looking for workers; it depends also on whether potential employees have the skills employers want, and have them in areas where the jobs are. For want of any other measure, in recent years economists have generally put the figure at 3 percent of the labor force, which was the average in 1952–53, when the economy was last at "full employment" for any length of time. (In fact, unemployment averaged 2.7 percent during the first three quarters of 1953.)

Some economists believe the frictional rate may have gone up since then. They point out that the proportion of women and teenagers in the labor force has increased; these groups move in and out of the labor force with greater frequency than adult men, and consequently have higher unemployment rates. And unemployment compensation and other social-insurance programs probably mean that workers are under less economic pressure to take the first job that comes along; they can pick and choose—which means longer spells between jobs.

These changes have been offset, however, by the dramatic rise in the educational level of the labor force. In general, the less education a person has, the fewer the jobs he is equipped to fill. Today there are only 16,500,000 workers who have not got beyond grammar school—six million fewer than in 1952. Such workers represent less than one-quarter of the labor force today, compared to nearly two-fifths in 1952. Because of this improvement in the quality of the labor force, and because workers are more mobile now than they used to be, the Council of Economic Advisers believes that the economy probably can operate efficiently at a lower unemployment rate now than it could in the early 1950s.

If the unemployment rate were to decline to 3 percent by the year's end, that would permit an 800,000 rise in employment over and above the growth in the labor force; cutting the rate to 2.7 percent would add still another 200,000. Thus a reduction in unemployment, combined with the growth of the labor force, would permit a rise in total employment between 2,000,000 and 2,500,000 over the course of 1966—versus a rise of 2,400,000 in the preceding twelve months.

Some of that increase was used up by the large buildup in employment during the first quarter of 1966; total employment in the quarter rose at an annual rate of between 3,000,000 and 3,600,000. The range reflects some uncertainties in the employment statistics, and these make it hard to explain the buildup satisfactorily. But whatever the reasons for the big first-quarter employment gains, some slowdown in the rate of increase now seems certain. It will reflect lesser growth rates of demand and output, particularly in manufacturing.* These rates will surely turn down; industrial production has jumped 6.5 percent since September 1965 in response to the buildup in defense contracts, but the force of that buildup has already been felt (barring a further major increase in our effort in Vietnam), and consumer spending will also increase more slowly. On balance, then, no further strain in the labor market seems likely; employers should not have significantly more difficulty finding new employees than they have encountered so far. It may well be, in fact, that the hardest adjustments have already been made.

The productivity picture

In short, the near-term manpower situation looks tolerably bright: a more or less normal growth in employment seems likely, and there is nothing in the labor-force data to suggest that excessive strains will be associated with the growth. However, the

* The slowdown began in May 1966, with the fall-off in auto sales.

prospect of strains cannot really be evaluated without looking at the recent pattern of productivity—i.e., output per man-hour.

Fortunately, there is no evidence that a serious slowdown in productivity is developing. The increase in output per man-hour in 1965 *was* smaller than that of the year before—2.8 percent for the private economy as a whole, versus 3.6 percent the year before. (In the nonfarm sector the rise was 2.4 percent versus 3.6 percent.) But that "lag" has to be seen in perspective: the productivity gains of 1964, like those of the three previous years, were extraordinary because business was putting idle plant and partly idle managerial and supervisory personnel to work.

The point can be seen clearly by considering a new index that was developed for *Fortune* by Alan Greenspan of Townsend-Greenspan & Co., consulting economists. The index measures the underlying trend in output per man-hour, extracting from the BLS figures those changes that can be attributed to changes in the economy's operating rate. What the index suggests is a surprising stability in the underlying trend: between 1960 and 1964, output per man-hour adjusted for changes in utilization increased by 3.3 percent a year—only fractionally above the postwar average. In other words, almost all that above-trend rise in productivity derived from the rise in the economy's operating rate.

Some decline in the productivity growth rate was inevitable, therefore, once the idle capacity had been put to use and firms were straining their facilities beyond the most efficient point; the 1965 decline was pretty much what might have been expected. But there is no reason to expect any further decline in 1966 as a result of overly high operating rates. New capacity coming on stream should ease some of the strain. And analysis of quarterly data for the private economy, based on unpublished BLS statistics, and for a group of manufacturing industries for which measures of physical output are available, indicates that the year-to-year lag was not part of any steady downward drift. On the contrary, the lag shown for the year involved: (1) sharp drops in productivity around midyear, when capacity was under pressure and some anticipatory hiring may have been going on; and (2) a partial but persistent recovery in the fall and winter. (The quarterly figures for the private economy as a whole put the low point in the second quarter; the monthly figures for the group of manufacturing industries suggest that the low was in the third quarter.) Tentative estimates of first-quarter 1966 productivity indicate gains of roughly the same order of magnitude as in the preceding quarter.

To be sure, there are a number of factors that make productivity gains harder to come by. Many of the new employees who will be added to payrolls this year are bound to be less efficient than established employees; and while training and supervision may offset some of this drag, they do involve costs—and productivity drags—of their own. Efficiency tends to drop, too, when firms add substantial overtime in the form of more hours or a sixth day of work; the fatigue level is greater, and absenteeism tends to increase. Labor discipline is likely to weaken when workers with any degree of skill know they can walk outside and get another job right away. Substantial overtime pay may also weaken work incentives. For example, a midwest machinery manufacturer operating a six-day shift has heavy absenteeism on Mondays; his employees feel they can afford to take the day off to go hunting, or just to loaf, since, with double pay for working Saturday, they still take home more than their normal paychecks.

Relieving the pressure

At very high rates of operation, moreover, productivity tends to suffer from the use of "standby" facilities, which are, in the nature of the case, older and less efficient than those normally used. At such times, furthermore, there is a drag on productivity from the introduction of *new* facilities. It usually takes some time to train a work force to use any new plant or new equipment; it may take even longer to "debug" the plant and get it working at peak efficiency. This debugging problem helps to explain why there is relatively less technological change in periods of high capital spending than in periods of low spending. When the spending is designed to bring on additional capacity in a hurry, the engineers are reluctant to install new and unfamiliar processes that may take a long time to debug; they prefer, instead, to stay with the existing state of the art.

In 1966, however, capital expenditures are likely to contribute more to raising than to lowering productivity. The huge outlays of 1963–65, as well as a portion of the 1966 outlays, will provide large additions to capacity—more than 7 percent in manufacturing in 1966, versus 6 percent in 1965—thus permitting a number of industries, including some of those under greatest pressure, to lower their operating rates to more efficient levels. One of the most encouraging aspects of the current situation, as the Council of Economic Advisers pointed out in its January 1966 report to the President, lies in the fact that the pressure on capacity is considerably less now than it was during the 1955–57 boom, when productivity lagged very badly and a great "cost-push" inflation set in.

We may also anticipate that productivity over-all will continue to be bolstered by a movement of employees away from lower-paying industries like agriculture, retail trade, domestic service, and personal services, and into manufacturing. From the standpoint of the manufacturing company, we have observed, the new workers are less productive than the old. But from the standpoint of the economy as a whole, the effect may be quite the opposite: in moving from low-productivity (hence low-paying) industries to relatively high-productivity (better-paying) industries, they tend to increase average output per man-hour. Indirectly, furthermore, this movement may tend to raise productivity in the industries left behind by these workers. A shift from trade to manufacturing, for example, is not likely to cause any loss in retail sales; the result is more likely to be a substantial increase in the average sales of the remaining employees. The real burden of the shift in this case is borne by the customers, who just have to wait longer for service.

The relaxed executives

In general, the executives interviewed by *Fortune* seemed remarkably relaxed about productivity (in sharp contrast with their grumbling about the "labor shortage"). Virtually all the executives reported that productivity was holding up well; most were pleased that labor turnover had not risen more than it had. (In February 1966 the seasonally adjusted "quit rate" for manufacturing firms was 2.4 percent, compared to 2.2 percent in the fourth quarter of 1965 and 1.7 percent a year before.)

Forecasts of changes in productivity are subject to even greater risks than those attendant on economic forecasts. Still, on the basis of the evidence now available, there seems to be little reason to expect the 1966 increase in output per man-hour to be substantially smaller (or larger for that matter) than the preceding year's. If this judgment is correct, the increase in output per man-hour is likely to fall in a range of perhaps 2 percent to 3 percent in 1966, the lower figure being the more likely if unemployment drops to 3 percent or below, the higher if the drop in unemployment is less than that.

Taking everything together, therefore, it would appear that business can live with the current "labor shortage," that it need not produce serious inflationary pressures. This judgment necessarily involves some subjective elements, and some economists may differ—including *Fortune*'s Business Roundup. There are uncertainties about the course of the war in Vietnam; other uncertainties have to do with the possibility of an "inflation psychology" taking hold among consumers. In the end, a lot will depend on businessmen themselves—on the efforts they make to adapt to a new kind of labor market. There are obvious reasons for them to make some very strenuous efforts to adapt.

APPENDIX

Statistics for the Charts

Table A-1. Long-Term Productivity Growth in the Private Economy,
1890–1964[a]

(gross private product per man-hour, 1947 = 100)

1890	30.1	1915	44.4	1940	81.8
1891	30.8	1916	47.7	1941	88.8
1892	32.6	1917	45.3	1942	90.2
1893	31.3	1918	48.9	1943	93.4
1894	31.5	1919	52.1	1944	100.7
1895	33.5	1920	51.7	1945	105.0
1896	32.7	1921	55.3	1946	99.6
1897	34.9	1922	54.8	1947	100.0
1898	35.4	1923	58.0	1948	103.5
1899	36.1	1924	60.5	1949	106.5
1900	36.7	1925	60.4	1950	114.1
1901	39.2	1926	62.1	1951	116.9
1902	37.8	1927	63.2	1952	119.5
1903	38.6	1928	63.2	1953	124.5
1904	38.5	1929	66.0	1954	126.7
1905	39.5	1930	64.3	1955	132.3
1906	42.5	1931	65.0	1956	132.4
1907	42.4	1932	62.7	1957	137.1
1908	40.3	1933	61.7	1958	140.5
1909	43.3	1934	69.0	1959	145.1
1910	42.5	1935	71.3	1960	148.0
1911	43.4	1936	74.8	1961	153.3
1912	44.2	1937	75.2	1962	159.8
1913	45.7	1938	77.8	1963	164.3
1914	42.7	1939	80.7	1964	170.5

[a] See Chart 1, p. 10.

Table A–2. Postwar Productivity Growth by Industry[a]

(*gross private product per man-hour, 1947 = 100*)

| | Goods industries | | | |
	Agriculture	*Mining*	*Manufacturing*	*Construction*
1947	100.0	100.0	100.0	100.0
1948	118.7	104.7	102.7	102.2
1949	113.2	108.4	105.0	106.1
1950	128.8	118.3	111.9	112.7
1951	127.6	124.8	113.9	113.4
1952	139.2	127.6	115.5	113.0
1953	155.0	133.1	121.1	115.6
1954	166.5	142.1	123.0	117.0
1955	171.2	148.6	130.8	118.3
1956	174.9	150.5	128.2	115.4
1957	186.3	152.5	132.1	116.3
1958	203.1	157.9	134.1	116.6
1959	202.4	161.7	139.4	115.9
1960	214.7	169.7	139.8	118.0
1961	229.1	182.8	143.9	120.2
1962	235.0	189.3	151.5	122.2
1963	257.6	197.0	154.9	123.3
1964	265.8	201.4	160.7	125.8

| | Service industries | | | |
	Utilities and communications	*Transportation*	*Trade*	*Other services*
1947	100.0	100.0	100.0	100.0
1948	102.6	102.9	99.5	102.5
1949	110.9	105.0	100.6	105.5
1950	121.1	120.3	110.7	105.1
1951	130.8	124.9	110.8	105.3
1952	138.6	125.5	114.7	107.6
1953	143.9	128.4	117.1	108.8
1954	155.2	130.9	116.6	110.1
1955	170.9	142.5	124.1	109.5
1956	180.3	145.2	124.6	112.5
1957	190.7	145.2	125.8	114.2
1958	204.6	148.1	125.1	117.6
1959	224.7	156.8	130.5	120.9
1960	237.3	162.4	129.4	123.0
1961	253.3	166.8	131.9	125.6
1962	269.9	175.6	137.3	128.3
1963	288.2	183.2	140.3	130.7
1964	303.3	191.0	145.2	134.1

[a] See Chart 2, p. 13.

Table A-3. Employment by Source of Demand[a]

(*millions of people*)

	Private sector	Nonprofit institutions	Government	Total Employed
1947	40.1	1.7	8.1	49.9
1950	40.3	1.9	9.1	51.3
1957	42.9	2.6	13.5	59.0
1962	43.3	3.2	15.6	62.1
1963	43.9	3.3	16.2	64.3
1964	45.0	3.5	16.5	65.0

[a] See Chart 3, p. 37.

Table A-4. Employment by Kind of Industry[a]

(*percent of total employment*)

	1869	1899	1929	1948	1964
Goods					
Agriculture	48.2	36.5	20.8	13.6	7.1
Manufacturing	17.7	20.1	22.3	27.3	26.3
All other	6.5	7.9	7.8	7.8	7.1
Services					
Government	3.1	3.7	6.2	9.2	13.4
Trade	7.8	10.8	17.0	18.3	18.9
All other	16.7	21.0	25.9	23.8	27.2

[a] See Chart 4, p. 38.

Table A-5. Net Change in Labor Force by Age Groups[a]

(*thousands of people*)

Age groups	1950–55	1955–60	1960–65	1965–70	1970–75
14–19	−61	864	1,302	1,039	758
20–24	−596	370	1,622	2,432	1,463
25–34	580	−655	−81	1,968	4,133
35–54	3,085	2,889	1,511	812	234
55 and over	1,146	763	877	1,392	1,059

[a] See Chart 5, p. 40.

140   APPENDIX

Table A–6. Unemployment Rates by Age Groups[a]

(*percent*)

	All ages	14–19	20–24	25–34	35–54	55 and over
1950	5.3	11.3	7.2	4.4	3.7	4.4
1951	3.3	7.7	3.6	2.6	2.3	2.9
1952	3.1	8.0	4.0	2.2	1.9	2.2
1953	2.9	7.1	4.0	2.1	1.8	2.2
1954	5.6	11.4	8.4	4.7	3.9	3.9
1955	4.4	10.2	6.3	3.5	3.0	3.7
1956	4.2	10.4	6.0	3.3	2.8	3.1
1957	4.3	10.8	7.1	3.9	3.2	3.4
1958	6.8	14.4	11.2	6.8	5.3	5.1
1959	5.5	13.2	8.5	5.0	4.2	4.4
1960	5.6	13.6	8.7	5.2	4.1	4.1
1961	6.7	15.2	10.4	6.2	5.1	5.3
1962	5.6	13.3	9.0	5.1	4.1	4.3
1963	5.7	15.6	8.8	5.2	3.9	4.1
1964	5.2	14.7	8.3	4.3	3.5	3.8
1965	4.6	13.6	6.7	3.7	3.0	3.1

[a] See Chart 6, p. 41.

Table A–7. Net Change in Number of Teenage Workers 1930–60[a]

(*thousands of people*)

	Male	Female	Total
Total	−140	260	120
Farm workers	−750	−150	−900
Laborers	50	− 30	20
Operatives	70	−230	−160
Craftsmen-technicians	80	20	100
Service workers	200	220	420
Clerical workers	0	330	330
Sales workers	210	100	310

[a] See Chart 7, p. 54.

Table A–8. How Quitting Early Can Shrink a Worker's Pension[a]

| Age at retirement | Monthly benefits | | |
	Private pension	Social Security	Total
50	$34.00		$34.00
51	36.00		36.00
52	38.30		38.30
53	40.70		40.70
54	43.40		43.40
55	46.30		46.30
56	49.50		49.50
57	53.10		53.10
58	56.90		56.90
59	61.20		61.20
60	66.00		66.00
61	71.30		71.30
62	77.30	$149.30	226.60
63	84.00	163.00	247.00
64	91.50	176.80	268.30
65	100.00	190.50	290.50

[a] See Chart 8, p. 72.

Table A–9. Average Annual Increase in Output Attributable
to Greater Productivity and Higher Employment[a]
(percent)

	Average annual increase in gross private product (constant dollars)	Average annual increase in output per man-hour	Change in employment
1947–57	3.8	3.4	0.4
1957–60	2.7	2.7	0
1960–65	4.7	3.6	1.1

[a] See Chart 9, p. 116.

Table A–10.   Labor Costs: The New Equation[a]
(*Index: 1960 = 100*)

	Output per man-hour	Compensation per man-hour	Unit labor costs
1947	65.8	50.2	76.4
1948	68.6	54.6	79.6
1949	70.8	55.6	78.5
1950	76.7	59.4	77.5
1951	78.9	65.3	82.8
1952	80.4	69.4	86.3
1953	83.7	73.8	88.2
1954	85.6	76.0	88.9
1955	89.4	78.4	87.7
1956	89.5	82.9	92.6
1957	92.2	88.3	95.8
1958	94.9	91.9	97.0
1959	98.4	96.2	97.9
1960	100.0	100.0	100.0
1961	103.4	103.7	100.3
1962	108.2	108.3	100.1
1963	112.0	112.5	100.5
1964	116.0	118.2	102.0
1965	119.2	122.8	102.9

[a] See Chart 10, p. 121.

Index

Haggstrom, Warren, 86
Heller, Walter, 95
Helstein, Ralph, 62
Hilton, Alice Mary, 6–7
Hiring standards, 50–51, 118–120, 122
Hofstadter, Richard, 106
Holidays, increased, 67
Hunter, Woodrow W., 65

Income: anti-poverty workers, 88–89; of early retirees, 70, 71, 72, 141; poverty statistics, 76–77; see also Wages
Industrial Areas Foundation, 82
Industry: demand, economy and, 36–37, 39; early retirement in, 62–65, 73–75; employment in, 38, 139; expansion, 39, 117–118; labor costs, 120, 121, 132, 142; labor surplus tapping, 122–125; productivity increases in, 138; tight labor market and, 119–120, 122; training employees, 125–127; see also specific industry, e.g., Manufacturing
Innis, Harold, 107

Jaffe, A. J., 52
Job Corps, 88
Johnson, Lyndon, 45, 76

Kennedy, John F., 45
Killingsworth, Charles C., 4–5
Kravitz, Sanford L., 78

Labor, elimination of human, 99–100
Labor costs, 120, 121, 132, 142; capital costs vs., 22
Labor force: age structure, 40, 41, 65–66, 69, 139; education level, 51–52, 129; frictional unemployment, 129–130; hiring standards, 50–51, 118–120, 122; increases, 43, 44, 62, 127–128, 129; industrial distribution, 38, 139; job competition, 49–50; occupational structure, 29–30, 32–33, 35, 52–56, 140; pool of available, 117–118; supply and demand, 31–32,

33, 122; teaching skills, 125–127; unfilled jobs, 31–32; utilization of available, 122–125; women in, 49–50, 65–66, 69, 123–124, 129; youth in, 45, 46–47, 48, 49, 52, 53, 55–57, 123, 129, 140; see also Demand for labor; Employment; Youth employment; and under specific topic, e.g., Production workers
Language, development of, 107–108
Larrabee, Eric, 45
Leisure, 67–68
Literacy, effects of, 108–110
Locke, Hubert, 93

MacDonald, Dwight, 109n
Mailer, Norman, 106
Management: cybernation and, 6; productivity views, 133–134
Manipulation, complexity of, 18–20
Manpower training programs, 84
Manufacturing: nonproduction workers in, 35–36; production workers in, 1, 35–36, 42–43; productivity in, 13–14, 130, 131–132, 133–134
Mayors, on poverty war, 79–82
McClure, Frank, 124
McLuhan, Marshall, 17, 97, 101–102, 103, 107–112
Mechanization of existing functions, 17–18
Medicare, 70
Mesthene, Emmanuel G., 112–113
Michael, Donald N., 1–2, 5–6, 7–8, 24
Middle class: bias of welfare, 83–86; youth and values of, 60–61
Miller, S. M., 59
Monetary and fiscal policy, economic growth and, 37, 39
Mosher, Ralph S., 19–20
Moynihan, Daniel P., 95

National Child Labor Committee, 46
National Committee on Employment of Youth, 46
Negroes: failure attitudes, 61; unemployment of, 27, 115